MIRACLE MAN

What People are Saying About *Miracle Man*

"This book eloquently delves into the profound odyssey of a seasoned veteran, imbued with both empathy and authenticity. It's an essential literary experience for those eager to grasp the intricacies of the warrior spirit."
~ S. E. Green, Bestselling Author

"Written from the heart of a warrior and the healing pen of a poet, Ferruolo brings us to the protagonist's shadows while refusing to let us avoid our own. *Miracle Man* is quite literally a comprehensive roadmap on our shared human journey to understanding the connectivity within each of us, between man and fellow man, earth and the Mystical."
~ Stephen Colcord, Retired US Marshall, Author, *Collateral Lead* & *Failure to Register*

"A philosophical and metaphysical journey from despair to hope, healing and enlightenment. It's like Jonathon Livingston Seagull for veterans. It may be a quick read, but it is filled with ancient wisdom and timeless truth. It's an important guide to healing, especially for veterans, wrapped within a compelling story."
~ WL Bach, Retired Navy SEAL, Author, *Black Dog Escape*

Miracle Man

DR. DAVE FERRUOLO

Tattered Script Publishing

Tattered Script Publishing
PO Box 1704
Middleburg, Virginia 20117
tatteredscript.com

ISBN 979-8-2183293-6-5
ISBN 978-0-9776412-5-3
Printed in the United States of America
10 9 8 7 6 5 4 3 2 1 0

Tattered Script Publishing: Crafting Cultural
Creativity and Authenticity

Cover art by Dr. Dave Ferruolo
Cover design by Emily Kallick

First Printing 2024

Contents

Author's Note   xi

The Brink of Despair   1

The Crash and Awakening   6

Ageless Wisdom   14

The Earth's Connection   21

The Journey Commences   28

The Girl and the Box   35

The Symphony of Lives & Living   48

The Mirror of Reflection   67

The Trials of the Soul   87

The Unfolding Path   96

The Silent Guide   102

The Convergence of Paths   110

The Awakening   115

The Final Journey   125

Epilogue   135

About The Author   137

Commitment to Veterans

A portion of the proceeds of *Miracle Man* will go to support non-profits that cater to facilitating psychedelic-assisted therapies for combat veterans.

Author's Note

In April 1997 the seeds of *Miracle Man* were sown, embarking on a journey that spanned decades. This narrative stood resilient through the passage of time, beckoning me back repeatedly, evolving with each revision. It has been sculpted and reshaped, witnessing transformations in style, plot, and character arcs. Yet, through these metamorphoses, one element remained unwavering: the tale of a former Navy SEAL swimming the treacherous waters of reintegration into the civilian world.

Often, the inquiry arises: is the first chapter rooted in truth? While it does not mirror my personal story, it resonates with the collective experience of numerous special forces combat veterans. The genesis of understanding their profound challenges came as I delved into my veteran-focused doctorate dissertation. It was within the scholarly depths that *Miracle Man* began to crystallize, gaining form and substance.

The completion of my academic endeavor shifted my gaze toward the remarkable realm of psychedelic-assisted therapies. Stories of profound change, shared by veterans and close comrades, illuminated the path. My journeys to psychedelic retreats with fellow warriors infused *Miracle Man* with life, culminating decades of transformative work. To me, this is a marvel of personal significance.

As you venture into this story, immerse yourself not just in the narrative but in the underlying message: Aaron Robert Gossy's journey mirrors many who have braved the battlefield, aiming to enlighten and entertain. May *Miracle Man* serve as a beacon of awareness and enjoyment, honoring the intricacies of veterans' experiences.

~ *Dr. Dave Ferruolo*

Your visions will become clear only when you can look into your own heart. Who looks outside, dreams; who looks inside, awakes.

~ Carl Jung

The Brink of Despair

In the restless darkness of his quarters, Aaron Robert Gossy lay awake, the ghosts of his past swirling like mist around him. A Navy SEAL Chief, Aaron's life had become a battleground where memories of war clashed with the mundane realities of civilian life. The unrelenting specters of PTSD, moral injury, depression, and an unquenchable thirst for alcohol haunted his days. At night, these demons sharpened their claws, dragging him towards the abyss of suicidal thinking.

His quarters were a stale, dimly lit space along the Southern California shorelines. It was both a refuge and a prison. Adorned with military accolades and fading photographs of comrades, the walls stood as silent witnesses to his internal turmoil. The faint glow of streetlights seeped through the blinds, casting long, somber shadows that danced mockingly around him.

Aaron's mind often wandered back to the battlegrounds, the sounds of gunfire and explosions echoing in his ears. He remembered the adrenaline, the fear, the camaraderie, and the unmistakable sense of purpose. But those memories were intertwined with darker ones —the loss of friends, the screams of the wounded, the faces of the enemy. These memories were his tormentors, relentless and unforgiving.

Amidst this chaos, there lurked a deeper yearning within Aaron, a whisper in the storm calling him towards a transformative journey. It was a quest for meaning, for healing, and a path to reclaim the fragments of his soul scattered across the sandboxes of the Middle East and buried in the depths of his despair. This yearning was the faint flicker of light in his darkness, the subtle but persistent notion that there was more to life, more to him than this relentless suffering.

Aaron pulled back the shades, his eyes reacting with a quick squint to the early rays of the Imperial Beach sunrise. His eyes traced the movements of the young sailors below. He watched them with admiration and a deep, aching nostalgia. The sight of these men, boys really, so full of life and determination, training to be part of Naval Special Warfare, was a reminder of his journey—a journey that now felt like a distant memory.

As he observed them, Aaron couldn't help but see his younger self in these trainees, full of vigor and unburdened by the scars of war. The Silver Strand training grounds became a living metaphor for his lost youth and the dreams he once harbored. Each leap from the tower, each triumphant landing, echoed the leaps of faith he had taken, only to land in a reality far removed from what he had envisioned.

Numerous military accolades, once a source of immense pride, now felt like heavy chains around his neck, mooring him to depths of guilt, shame, and hopelessness. Peering at the two purple hearts on the floor, his thoughts churned like a tempest, a relentless assault of haunting memories and unspoken regrets. Shadows of the past waged war in the recesses of his mind, each echo a piercing reminder of battles fought and the price paid. In the quiet of his room, the ghosts of fallen comrades whispered tales of sacrifice, their voices a chorus of guilt and unresolved grief.

The bottle became his only ally in this private hell, a liquid reprieve from the relentless siege within. Each sip was a temporary ceasefire, a fleeting moment of numbness amid chaos. Yet, as the amber liquid dwindled, so too did the respite it offered, leaving him more desolate in its wake.

As the day waned, Aaron found himself again seeking refuge in the familiar embrace of bourbon. The burn of the drink was a welcome pain, a tangible sensation against the intangible torment of his soul. Slowly, the world around him blurred, and the sharp edges of reality softened until he slipped into a state of oblivion, a bourbon-induced catatonia that had become his daily ritual of escape.

The confusion of lost hours was a permeating fog in his brain. He woke, barely comprehending the darkness that meant night. He peered around his quarters, a dank space that felt more like a cell than a home. The walls were adorned with reminders of a life that now seemed alien to him—medals, commendations, photos of his platoon. Instead of bringing a sense of pride, each item only deepened his sense of loss and disconnection.

In the solitude of his room, Aaron's gaze fell upon his revolver, an object that had become a symbol of protection and destruction. His hand trembled as he picked it up, feeling the cold, metallic weight. He opened the cylinder, watching it spin, five empty chambers of the available six, a haunting metaphor for the void he felt within himself.

At that moment, Aaron stood at the precipice, grappling with the darkest corners of his mind. The spinning of the revolver's cylinder mirrored the spinning of his thoughts - chaotic, dizzying, and dangerously close to the edge. The idea of ending his pain with a single decisive act was both terrifying and alluring. Click. Nothing.

The fall of the hammer echoed in the room, a sound both jarring and strangely soothing. It was the sound of life persisting despite the darkness that threatened to engulf him. Aaron teetered on the edge of oblivion in that harrowing moment, his fate resting on the randomness of a spinning revolver cylinder.

Wracked with emotion, his body crumpled to the floor. Curling into a fetal position, his sobs breaking the oppressive silence of the room. Every tear that traced his cheek bore silent witness to wars waged on distant lands and those that raged within the confines of his mind. Clutching the revolver in one hand and his two Purple Hearts in the other, he was a portrait of a warrior at his most vulnerable, grappling with the complexities of valor and the haunting specter of despair.

The reality of his situation weighed heavily on him. Tomorrow marked the end of his time in the Navy, the closing of a chapter that had defined him for so long. He was to be medically discharged, no longer a soldier, but a broken man, out of options. The journey back to his hometown loomed ahead, a transition filled with uncertainty. He would be catching a military flight, leaving behind the life he knew—stepping into an unknown darkness.

As he lay there on the floor, Aaron's exhausted body succumbed to sleep. The turmoil of the day, the intense confrontation with his mortality, had drained him of all energy. But not his life.

The Crash and Awakening

Aaron trudged towards the C-130, his boots scuffing the same gravel paths that bright-eyed and steadfast recruits now marched. He watched them, a pang of nostalgia mingling with a bitter sense of loss. Their laughter and banter, so full of life and purpose, contrasted sharply with the emptiness gnawing at his soul. He had once been one of them, full of vigor and a sense of invincibility. Now, as he walked away from the life that had defined him, each step felt like a descent into an unknown abyss.

His journey to the aircraft was silent, marked by the heavy burden of his duffel bag and the heavier weight of his memories. The compound, bustling with activity, felt like a world apart. The sky above was a stage for the young trainees, parachutes blossoming like hope against the clear blue. Aaron watched them, their descent a poignant reminder of his first jump—a leap into the unknown that now felt like a lifetime ago.

The C-130 loomed ahead, its massive frame casting a long shadow over the tarmac. It symbolized his years of service, a familiar giant that had whisked him away to distant lands and dangerous missions. Yet, as he approached, his steps faltered. This was no ordinary flight; it was a final farewell to a life he had known, a life that had shaped and, in many ways, shattered him.

Once embodying strength and determination, the aircraft now seemed a forbearing sign of finality. The whir of engines and the hustle of the ground crew resonated with conclusiveness. Aaron hesitated at the foot of the ramp, his heart heavy with a tumult of emotions. The thought of boarding for the last time, of severing the last physical tie to his Frogman identity, filled him with an inexplicable dread.

Memories flooded his mind, unbidden and relentless. He remembered the exhilaration of combat, the bonds forged in the heat of battle, and the laughter and camaraderie that made the forward operating bases feel like home. But these memories were intertwined with darker, more insidious ones—the screams of the wounded, the faces of the fallen, the moral quandaries that haunted his nights. These were the scars that medals couldn't heal, the invisible wounds that clung to his soul.

Each recollection was like a wave crashing over him with a force that left him breathless. The echoes of gunfire, the smell of cordite, the unyielding feelings of tension that never quite abated—it all came rushing back, a relentless tide of post-combat trauma that gnawed at his peace. And with it came the moral injury, the heavy burden of actions taken, and the decisions made in the unforgiving torment of war. They were ghosts whispering of guilt and loss, shadows lurking in his mind's corners.

As he finally climbed aboard, the interior of the C-130 offered no respite. The cavernous space, once a sanctuary, now felt like a capsule hurtling him toward an uncertain future. The chatter of the crew, the clatter of equipment being stowed—it all seemed distant, muffled by the rushing sound of his thoughts.

Aaron found his seat, the fabric worn and familiar under his touch. He sat there, surrounded by the ghosts of his past and the echoes of his present, teetering on the edge of an abyss that yawned wide and deep, beckoning him into a future he could neither see nor fathom. In this moment, suspended between what was and what would be, Aaron faced the most daunting mission of his life—the journey into the unknown.

Inside the aircraft, the banter and routine checks of the crew were a distant hum to Aaron. He sought refuge in a secluded spot at the back, strapping himself away from prying eyes. Here, he could surrender to his hangover-induced fatigue, his head buzzing with the cocktail of emotions that had kept him awake for nights on end. Aaron's eyes shuttered in this hidden corner, seeking solace in the embrace of sleep—a decision that would unwittingly become his salvation. As his eyelids moved to seal out the flickering lights of the C-130—his last glance was of his green flight duffel, tattered, worn, with faded initials, A.R. Gossy.

Initially as mundane as any other, the flight transformed abruptly into a nightmare. Aaron was jolted from his uneasy sleep and thrust into a world where the rules of reality no longer applied. Once a steady beast of steel and precision, the aircraft buckled and shrieked as if in agony. Violent turbulence seized the aircraft, tossing it about like a toy in the hands of a capricious storm.

Aaron's body, strapped securely to his makeshift berth, became a prisoner to the merciless shaking. His mind, still fogged with sleep, struggled to comprehend the chaos. The roar of the engines escalated into a deafening crescendo, battling against the screeching of metal that twisted and contorted under unimaginable stress. The sounds were not just heard but felt—a visceral symphony of destruction that vibrated in Aaron's very bones.

Around him, the world was a blur of motion and terror. The once orderly interior of the cargo area transformed into a maelstrom of flying equipment and dislodged cargo. The screams of fear from the personnel aboard merged with the cacophony, a human note to the hellish chorus that engulfed them. Aaron's training screamed at him to act, but he was a spectator, strapped down and powerless, his fate tied to the plummeting aircraft.

As the plane spiraled downwards, each second stretched into an eternity. Aaron's mind raced through every possible outcome, each grimmer than the last. He thought of his comrades, his family, the life he was leaving behind, but also of the pain and suffering that would instantly cease upon impact. The overwhelming force of the descent pressed him into his seat, a crushing reminder of his mortality. Aaron let out a loud maniacal laugh, then relaxed and closed his eyes. Slightly smirking, he welcomed the coming end.

The impact was instantaneous and eternal. The earth rose to meet them with a fury that no human engineering could withstand. The C-130 hit the sloped ground, its integrity succumbing in an instant. The world exploded into a blinding inferno of fire and smoke, a cataclysmic end to a journey that had barely begun.

Secured tightly in his isolated nook at the back of the plane, Aaron was shielded from the worst of the impact. The searing heat from the flames enveloped him, singeing his skin and scorching his lungs. The air was thick with the acrid smell of burning fuel and charred metal, a noxious cocktail that threatened to suffocate him. His ears rang with the echo of the crash, a haunting reminder of the chaos that had just unfolded.

In the midst of the inferno, a surreal sight caught Aaron's eye—hundreds of hundred-dollar bills, part of the aircraft's precious cargo, fluttering around him. They danced in the hot air, some alighting on the flames and catching fire themselves. It was a bizarre and grotesque display, symbolizing wealth and power reduced to ash in the face of nature's unforgiving might.

Trapped in his seat, Aaron struggled fiercely against the restraints that both saved and imprisoned him. His hands, blistered and trembling, worked frantically on the straps, an act of survival in the midst of chaos. The pain from his injuries—a mélange of burns, cuts, and fractures—was a distant echo against the adrenaline surging through his veins. With a final, desperate tug, he freed himself, tumbling into the remains of the fuselage.

The back of the aircraft, where Aaron had sought refuge, lay grotesquely twisted on the steep slope of a mountainside. The crash had torn it away from the main inferno, sparing his life by mere feet. Dazed, Aaron clung to the jagged metal, suspended precariously over a vertiginous drop that led to the riverbed below.

Every breath was agony. The inhalation of scalding smoke turned each inhale into a searing torment. His body was a tapestry of pain—first, second, and third-degree burns marred his skin, open wounds wept, his ribs cracked with each labored breath, and his leg, broken and useless, dangled beneath him.

Summoning a reservoir of strength he didn't know he possessed, Aaron fought against the pull of unconsciousness. He knew he had mere moments before the rest of the plane succumbed to the inferno. With tremendous effort, he pushed himself away from the wreckage, his body falling free.

The descent was a blur of pain and disorientation. He bounced off the remnants of the fuselage, each impact a burst of excruciating pain, before rolling helplessly down the embankment. Rocks and debris tore at his flesh, each jolt a reminder of his precarious grip on life. Then, with a final, graceless tumble, he fell over a small drop-off, landing in the shallow, cold waters of the river.

Aaron lay semi-submerged, his consciousness waning. The world around him, filled with the turmoil of heat, smoke, and the sharp scent of blood, blurred into an indistinct background. His mind was caught between the unstable edges of reality and vivid hallucinations. He struggled to distinguish between the two as hazy visions of fire, water, trees, and unusually large toads floated before his stinging eyes.

In his wavering moments of awareness, a figure emerged through the smoky heat haze and the distant flashing of red lights. It was a man, maybe a tribal elder, approaching with a calm, deliberate pace that defied the surrounding anarchy. *Am I dead?* Aaron thought.

Was this a hallucination, a trick of his tormented mind, or a guide to lead him to the other side? The elder's eyes, deep and knowing, met Aaron's. In them, Aaron saw the promise of salvation and truths yet uncovered. *I am dead?* He relinquished. Aaron perceived a resonant and strangely comforting sound—the rhythmic chorus of toads, their croaks, a song of life in the dense wilderness. He thought again, *Am I dead?* Yet, as he lay there, a subtle tug at his neck brought him back to the harsh and very painful reality. It was the dog tag chain, gently unraveled by unseen hands. A voice, both assuring and firm, broke the silence, "Rest Easy, Mr. A.R. Gossy. Help is on its way."

Ageless Wisdom

In the aftermath of the crash, Aaron's existence blurred into a haze of pain and semi-consciousness. His battered body, a canvas of unseen injuries, lay surrendered to the merciless elements. His dog tag's faint, familiar weight pressed against his chest, a metallic whisper of his identity amidst the chaos.

Aaron's senses were assaulted by unrelenting discomfort as his mind teetered on the edge of awareness. Sharp headaches pulsed through his temples, uninvited and relentless. A pitched ringing in his ears reverberated through his semi-conscious state, a dissonant reminder of an unseen affliction. Simultaneously, a tightness gripped his chest, each heartbeat a resonant echo in the void of his fragmented reality.

His phoenix tattoo, its wings spread wide amidst a dance of flames, seemed to throb with a life of its own. The skin around the vibrant ink felt unusually sensitive, itching and aching in a rhythm mirroring his pulsating discomforts. This emblem of rebirth and resurgence starkly contrasted his current vulnerability, a paradoxical symbol of strength in the face of adversity.

Interwoven with these physical sensations was the toads' persistent, strangely comforting chorus. This rhythmic serenade, so out of place yet oddly harmonious with his predicament, offered a surreal backdrop to his plight.

Though seemingly disconnected, these elements collectively hinted at a deeper, underlying reality. Unbeknownst to Aaron, these sensations were the threads of a revelation, a prelude to an awakening that would bridge the chasm between this death-teetering journey and a truth yet to be discovered.

For just shy of six weeks, time lost its meaning for Aaron. The elder used elixirs derived from the earth—potent concoctions of herbs, reptile venoms, and secret ingredients known only to indigenous cultures. These healing agents, steeped in tradition and the primal knowledge of the earth, worked not only on Aaron's physical wounds but also on his psyche. The elder's chants and prayers, a rhythmic backdrop to the healing process, seemed to reach into the very core of Aaron's being.

In this altered state, Aaron's journey within himself unfolded like a primal dance of existence. Each dose of the potent elixir, administered by the elder with the solemnity of a sacred rite, pulled Aaron deeper into his psyche's uncharted territories. The experience was not just a venture into the cradle of light but a pilgrimage into the depths of his consciousness, akin to an ancient shamanic communion with the divine.

Aaron's reality became fluid, transcending tangible forms and flowing with cosmic tides. His visions, neither purely terrifying nor solely ecstatic, charted a path through his subconscious, revealing the myriad paths of his life. This introspection brought him face-to-face with his past as a child and a soldier, the camaraderie amidst violence, and the brutality of war that had left indelible scars on his soul.

Each sacrament intensified this experience, enveloping Aaron in a powerful vibratory force that stripped away the room's meditative ambiance. His journey became a profound exploration of contrasts—light against dark, being against non-being. This phase was a tribulation of self-inquiry, stretching each moment into eternity, asking him to confront the shadows within, his deepest fears, and recognize his resilience.

Aaron grappled with a visceral claustrophobia, an acute constriction that seemed to compress the universe upon his chest. This wasn't a metaphorical sensation but a brutally physical one, squeezing the life from his lungs, a psychological crucible where each breath became a Herculean task against the weight of creation bearing down upon him.

In these moments, Aaron faced the terror of annihilation, confronting the imposing possibility of non-existence. The only way through this maelstrom of fear was complete surrender, a letting go so profound that it felt akin to a small death, dissolving his ego in the face of the infinite. This surrender was not just mental but a capitulation of spirit and body.

Through this release, the dichotomy of light and darkness merged into a singular, boundless expanse. Aaron's physical limitations dissolved, and he became a consciousness unbound by mortality, immersed in the totality of existence, merging with the infinite, expanding into the grand expanse of the cosmos.

The transformation was not merely a chapter in his life; it rewrote his entire existence. Fear, negativity, and the burdens of his past dissolved into a newfound purity of existence—a rebirth that attuned his consciousness to a deeper resonance, forever altering his engagement with the world.

This experience transcended the visual, touching the fundamental nature of existence. Aaron found himself annihilated and reborn, a witness to the death of old paradigms and the birth of a profound inner peace. It was a dance of creation and destruction, a storm yielding to calm.

Reflecting on this journey, Aaron realized it was not an escape but a deeper penetration into reality's essence, highlighting the potential of psychedelics to catalyze profound personal growth. The experience was life-affirming, offering a glimpse into the boundless potential of the human spirit to connect, transform, and transcend.

The transformation echoed the metamorphosis of a caterpillar into a butterfly. Once destructive and earth-bound, the caterpillar is reborn as an ethereal embodiment of grace and harmony. Similarly, Aaron's neural pathways, those well-trodden roads formed through a lifetime of habit, expanded, offering glimpses of a transformed existence. Yet, his former self's deeply ingrained patterns persisted, clinging to his psyche.

In this personal excursion, Aaron navigated the tension between past, present, and future selves. This journey was one of acceptance, embracing every aspect of his transformation with compassion, without the burden of expectation. It was a process of letting go of preconceived outcomes, severing attachments to potential futures, and becoming an act of liberation. Aaron learned to reside in a state of fluidity and curiosity, welcoming the unknown and fully embracing change.

During these 960 hours, Aaron experienced a recurring motif of death and rebirth, each bringing a terrifying yet exhilarating sense of dissolution followed by a rebirth into ecstatic oneness. He learned to look forward to these cycles, not with fear, but with anticipation for the profound peace and freedom they brought. The ecstasy of connection counterbalanced the terror of annihilation, each cycle a microcosm of his ongoing transformation.

As he relived the memories of his time in combat, Aaron faced a deep reckoning with his actions. He saw the faces of those he fought, the collateral damage of war, and the lives irreparably changed by his decisions. These visions forced him to confront the moral complexity of his past, the decisions made in the heat of battle, the haunting aftermath of those choices, the dead left behind, and the waves of lives ruined. It was a confrontation that demanded acceptance and forgiveness, both of others and, crucially, of himself.

In the depths of this profound introspection, Aaron began to understand the nature of his trauma and guilt. He grappled with moral injury, the inner conflict arising from violating one's ethical and moral code. The entheogenic elixirs enabled him to approach these heavy burdens with a new perspective, to see them not as unchangeable stains on his soul but as experiences that could be understood, processed, and ultimately integrated into his being.

The intense, often overwhelming nature of these experiences was balanced by moments of profound peace and insight. Aaron felt a connection to the world around him that transcended the physical—a sense of oneness with nature, humanity, and the universe itself. This connection brought with it a sense of liberation, a freedom from the constraints of his previous worldview.

Aaron's philosophical outlook began to shift dramatically. He started to perceive the world not as a series of isolated events and individuals but as an interconnected web, where every action and life had significance and impact. This realization brought a new sense of responsibility and purpose, a desire to live harmoniously with the world around him.

As Aaron emerged from this journey, transformed in body, mind, and spirit, he found himself at a crossroads. He was acutely aware of the choice that lay before him: to revert to the familiarity of his past self or to embrace the profound changes he had undergone and step forward into a new way of being.

The Earth's Connection

The ever-watchful elder guided Aaron through this tumultuous awakening. He spoke of the interconnectedness of all things, of the earth, sky, and the rivers that flowed with the lifeblood of the planet. The teachings were simple yet profound, imbuing Aaron with a newfound respect and awe for the natural world.

Aaron embarked on a journey of physical and spiritual healing under the elder's tutelage. Over four months, he learned to draw strength from the earth, to listen to the whispers of the wind, and to see the world with more than just his eyes. He discovered the healing power of meditation, the clarity that came with silence, and the wisdom inherent in every rock, tree, and creature.

The elder taught him ancient practices that connected him to the rhythms of the universe. He learned to meditate under the vast canopy of stars, to understand the language of birds, and to feel the earth's pulse beneath his feet. These lessons were about healing his body and opening his mind and soul to a broader understanding of existence.

Aaron's recovery was slow but steady. With each passing day, he grew stronger, his broken body forging back together, aided by the natural remedies and the nurturing environment. But it was his spirit that underwent the most profound transformation. He began to see the world through a different lens, recognizing the sacredness in all life.

With his deep-set eyes and weathered face, the elder became more than a healer to Aaron; he was a mentor, a spiritual guide who led him through the maze of his psyche. He taught Aaron about the cycles of life and death, the impermanence of all things, and the importance of living in harmony with the world.

As the days turned into weeks and weeks into months, Aaron's journey of self-discovery and healing continued. The rugged, mountainous landscape around him served as a physical and spiritual backdrop for this transformation. Each sunrise brought new lessons, and each sunset reflected the day's learnings.

The elder's teachings were not confined to words alone. They were embedded in the daily rituals of living in harmony with nature. Aaron learned to forage for food, identifying plants and herbs that held healing properties. He was taught the art of making medicines from these natural resources, understanding the delicate balance of elements that made them effective.

In the quiet moments of dawn, Aaron practiced yoga and tai chi, movements that aligned his body and spirit with the rhythm of the earth. Once foreign to him, these practices became a source of strength and inner peace.

The elder also introduced Aaron to many sacred ceremonies. They would sit around the fire under the starlit sky, and the elder would share stories of his ancestors, tales of courage, wisdom, and connection to the spirit world. These stories were not just narratives, but teachings imbued with the culture's deep understanding of life's mysteries.

As Aaron's physical strength returned, so did his mental clarity. The psychological wounds of his past, while not entirely healed, began to lose their grip. He looked at his experiences as a soldier from a new perspective, seeing the bravery and sacrifices but also recognizing the need for forgiveness and compassion—toward others and, more importantly, toward himself.

Sensing Aaron's growing understanding, the elder delved deeper into the teachings of interconnectedness. He spoke of the earth as a living, breathing entity of which they were both a part. He taught Aaron to listen to the whispers of the earth, to understand its joys and sorrows, and to see himself as a guardian of its balance.

Through these teachings, Aaron developed a profound connection to the world around him. He felt a kinship with the trees, the rivers, and the animals. He learned to move with purpose and respect for all forms of life. This connection extended beyond the physical; it was a spiritual awakening, an understanding of his place in the grand tapestry of existence.

The elder's wisdom also extended to the cosmos. He taught Aaron about the stars and the moon, the cycles of the planets, and their influence on the earth. They would spend nights gazing at the sky, the elder pointing out constellations and sharing their significance in the lore of his people.

As Aaron's understanding deepened, so did his questions. He began to ponder the bigger mysteries of life—its purpose, the nature of the soul, the journey after death. The elder answered these queries not with definitive answers but with guidance, provoking Aaron to seek his own truths.

One day as they sat by the river, the elder spoke of life as a continuous flow, like the water before them. "You have faced death, Aaron, and you have been reborn. But remember, the river does not cease to exist when it merges with the ocean. It becomes part of something vast, something infinite." Aaron glanced at his now very metaphorical tattoo. The exquisitely inked phoenix seemed alive, beckoning to detach and fly off his arm.

This lesson struck a chord in Aaron. "I have literally risen from the ashes," he replied, still gazing at the elegant yet very itchy tattoo. He realized that his journey was about healing from the past and embracing a future interconnected with the world around him. He began to see his life as a river with twists and turns, rapids, and calm stretches, leading toward an endless sea of possibilities.

As the months passed, Aaron's transformation became evident in his thoughts, words, and very being. He moved with a grace and awareness that spoke of his deep connection to the earth and its rhythms. The anger and confusion that had once clouded his mind gave way to a sense of purpose and peace.

The elder, watching Aaron's evolution, knew the time was approaching for their paths to diverge. He had imparted his wisdom, and now it was up to Aaron to continue the journey, armed with the lessons he had learned.

On the last night before Aaron's departure, they sat once more around the fire. The elder looked at Aaron, a hint of a smile on his weathered face. "Remember, Aaron, you are not just a part of this world; you are its caretaker. The wisdom you have gained here is not just for you; it is to be shared and spread like the seeds of the plants we have nurtured."

Aaron nodded, a sense of responsibility settling in his heart. He understood that his journey was not ending but merely changing course. He was no longer just a soldier or a survivor; he was a seeker, a guardian of the earth, and a vessel of the wisdom he had been given.

As the first light of dawn painted the sky in hues of orange and pink, Aaron stepped out of the modest shelter that had been his haven for the past months. He felt a sense of urgency, a need to share his gratitude and newfound insights with the elder who had guided him through his transformative journey. But as he looked around the familiar landscape, he realized something was amiss. At that moment, a sudden, piercing headache struck him like a bolt of lightning, leaving him momentarily disoriented. A high-pitched tone pierced his ears, a sound that seemed to emerge from the depths of the silence around him. Through the searing pain, he searched for the familiar.

The elder's presence, as constant as the rising sun, was nowhere to be found. Aaron searched the area, his heart sinking with each passing moment as the crescendo of ringing lingered. Then, a sharp, pressuring pain clenched his chest, a fleeting yet intense reminder of his vulnerability. Aaron fell to his knees, nonetheless intent on connecting with his healer.

The elder's possessions, the small tokens of his existence, were all gone. In their place, left behind as if in silent farewell, was an old Ford pickup truck, standing alone in the quiet of the morning. It struck Aaron as symbolic, reminiscent of the gift of a horse, a means to journey onward. The sensations, as sudden and mysterious as they were, ebbed away, leaving him in a profound stillness, breathing deeply and pondering the journey ahead.

Compelled by a mix of confusion and curiosity, Aaron approached the truck. Tucked haphazardly between several boxes in the back, he found a note. The handwriting was familiar, the message brief but profound. "I believe this is yours," it read. With apprehension and wonder, Aaron pushed back the old tarp covering the boxes.

There, amidst the dust and the memories of days spent exploring old mineshafts with the elder, were tattered boxes filled with bundles of hundred-dollar bills. It took Aaron a moment to process the sight, the reality of what lay before him. These were the remnants of the crash, the cargo destined for a purpose now lost to the winds of fate and time.

Aaron turned his gaze toward the rising sun, its rays beginning to warm the cool morning air. He shook his head, a smile playing on his lips. The irony of the situation wasn't lost on him—the wealth he had once guarded with his life now returned to him unexpectedly at a time when his values and perspective on life had shifted so profoundly.

Standing there, alone yet not lonely, gazing into the horizon where the sun ascended over the mountains, Aaron knew it was a new day, a new beginning. With the elder's final, enigmatic gift and the lessons he had learned, Aaron was ready to embark on the next phase of his journey. A journey not just of physical distance but of continued spiritual and emotional growth.

The Journey Commences

With its majestic ascent, the sun brought the dawn of a new chapter in Aaron's life. With the wisdom of the Indian elder etched into his soul, he embarked upon his *Argosy*, a journey transcending physical boundaries, delving into the realms of spiritual enlightenment and self-transformation. Each mile Aaron drove was a stride away from his past and into a realm of endless possibilities.

For the first week of his journey, Aaron wandered through a landscape of change and constancy, the natural world around him a mirror to the tumultuous thoughts swirling within. The elixirs given by the elder had set him on a path of profound introspection and awakening, yet as the days passed, a shadow of doubt began to creep into his mind. Was the transformation he experienced real or merely an illusion fostered by the potent substances?

As he traveled through dense forests and over rugged hills, the echo of the elder's teachings mingled with the chorus of nature, yet questions besieged his heart. The vivid clarity and connection to the universe he had felt under the elder's guidance now seemed like a distant dream, fading with each passing day. He couldn't shake off the feeling that the profound insights he had gained were slipping through his fingers like grains of sand.

Aaron grappled with the notion that perhaps the elixirs were the sole source of his enlightenment, and without them, he was regressing to his former self. The idea was unsettling, shaking the foundations of the spiritual edifice he had started to construct in his mind. But as he journeyed onward, a subtle yet significant realization dawned upon him—the transformation was not wearing off; it was evolving, taking root deep within him.

He began to understand that the elixirs were merely catalysts, initiators of a process that had to be nurtured and developed from within. The true essence of his transformation lay not in the substances themselves but in how they had opened his eyes to the latent potential of his spirit.

Aaron's connection to his inner self grew stronger with each passing day. The doubts and fears that had clouded his thoughts started dissipating, giving way to a renewed sense of purpose and clarity. He recognized that the journey he had embarked was not just about seeking answers from the external world but also about exploring the uncharted territories of his being.

As the first week of his journey neared its end, Aaron found himself on the outskirts of a small town, a bustling contrast to the secluded wilderness he had journeyed. The town, bustling with life and activity, was vibrant with the energy of everyday existence. It was here, amidst the cacophony of human life, that Aaron's journey, unbeknownst to him, would take an unexpected turn.

The town was a living, breathing entity, its streets pulsing with the rhythm of life. Marketplaces brimmed with vendors selling exotic spices and colorful textiles, their shouts harmonizing with the playful banter of children running through the narrow alleys. Temples and shrines stood as silent sentinels, bearing witness to the spiritual undercurrent that flowed beneath the surface of this unique community.

Aaron felt a sense of connection to the people around him as he walked the streets. Their lives reflected the diverse experiences that shaped the human condition. In this setting, vibrant and full of contrasts, Aaron's journey of self-discovery would continue to unfold, each encounter and experience a single step on his quest for enlightenment.

As Aaron wandered, his attention was captivated by the murals adorning the walls. Each painting told a story, a tribute to the heroes of old, their deeds immortalized in vibrant colors. Against this backdrop of myth and legend, he first saw the slumped blanket-laden shape, with wild silver-grey hair obscuring an aged face.

Seated beneath an ancient oak tree, the woman seemed almost a part of the landscape. Her eyes, deep pools of knowledge and mystery, met Aaron's gaze with an intensity that spoke volumes. She was dressed simply, with clothes worn but clean and a demeanor that of someone who had walked the earth for centuries, gathering wisdom with each step.

Aaron felt a connection, a sense of kinship with the elderly woman. He recognized in those wise eyes a reflection of his journey, a shared understanding of life's trials and tribulations. Compelled by a force greater than mere curiosity, Aaron approached her, his heart open to the lessons this chance encounter might impart.

"Good morning," Aaron greeted, his voice echoing the rising sun's warmth.

She looked up, her face breaking into a smile that crinkled the corners of her eyes. "Morning indeed, young traveler. What brings you to my humble abode?"

Aaron sat beside the woman, feeling the ancient bark of the oak against his back. "I'm on a journey," he began, "A quest for understanding—for transformation."

The woman nodded as if she had heard such declarations a thousand times before. "And what have you learned so far on this quest of yours?"

Aaron pondered the question, his mind tracing the events that had led him to this moment. "I've learned that wisdom often comes from the most unexpected places and that strength is found not in certainty but in embracing the unknown."

A spark of interest flickered in her deep, dark eyes. "Ah, the wisdom of uncertainty. A valuable lesson indeed." She paused, her gaze drifting to the bustling street. "But tell me, young traveler, are you prepared to face the challenges of such a journey?"

Aaron felt a surge of resolve. "I am. Whatever trials lie ahead...I am ready to face them."

The aged woman smiled again, her expression one of gentle amusement. "Very well. Then perhaps you can assist me with a dilemma of my own."

Intrigued, Aaron leaned in closer. "What kind of dilemma?"

"It's a matter of great importance," she began, her voice taking on a serious tone. "You see, I am in possession of a rare artifact, a relic of immense significance for those who once possessed it. However, its true meaning can only be known by a *rightful* owner after embarking on a journey such as yours."

Aaron's interest was piqued. "What kind of artifact? And why me?"

With a knowing gaze that seemed to transcend time, the old woman reached into the folds of her blanket and produced a small, intricately carved box. "This," she said, offering it to Aaron, "is a vessel of ageless lore, a fragment of the eternal cosmos that holds our existence. It's not just an artifact; it's a legacy, one I believe you're destined to unveil."

Aaron hesitated, feeling the profound weight of the old woman's words. This encounter was more than mere happenstance; it tested his resolve and dedication to his chosen path. As he took the box, a jolt of recognition sparked within him, a fleeting sense of familiarity that teased at the edges of his memory. It was as though the box was not just an object to be unlocked but a piece of a puzzle intimately connected to him—not something new, but something to remember.

The box was a marvel of craftsmanship, its surface a masterpiece of transformation and journey. The carvings depicted scenes of nature's relentless cycle of creation and destruction, the cosmos in its infinite dance of stars and galaxies, and amidst it all, an ancient sailing vessel —the Argosy—coursing through tumultuous seas under a watchful sun. The scenes spoke of change, unknown paths, and the endless voyage of discovery.

Aaron's voice was barely a whisper, awash with awe and curiosity, "How do I unlock it?" The question was not merely about the mechanism that sealed the box but the deeper mystery it represented—the unlocking of truths long hidden and intertwined destinies. The woman's enigmatic smile suggested that the answer lay not in a simple key or code, but in the journey Aaron was yet to undertake, a journey that would reveal the box's secrets as much as it would unveil his own.

The sagely elder leaned in, her eyes alight with a mysterious fire. "That, young traveler, is for you to discover. The key lies within you, in the lessons you've learned and the wisdom you've gained. Trust your instincts, and the path will reveal itself. As you resurrect, evolve, and remember who you are meant to be."

Aaron nodded, a sense of confused determination filling him. He knew this was no ordinary task. It was a pivotal moment in his journey, a step toward understanding the deeper truths of existence.

As he turned the box over in his hands, examining its intricate design, he felt a connection to something greater than himself, a sense of being part of a timeless narrative that spanned the ages. This was more than a physical journey; it was a voyage into the depths of his soul.

With the box in his possession, Aaron thanked the woman. With a warm embrace, he bid farewell and continued on his way, his mind alive with possibilities. He knew that the path ahead would be fraught with challenges, but he also knew that he was no longer the same man who had embarked on this journey. He had grown, transformed by the trials he had faced and the wisdom he had gained.

Aaron continued each step with the ancient box in hand, a commitment to his quest for enlightenment. The journey was far from over, but he was ready for whatever lay ahead, his heart open to the lessons of the universe and his spirit attuned to the mysteries of existence.

The Girl and
the Box

A metaphor for life's endless dramas, the town unfolded before Aaron like a vibrant painting. Its streets, pulsing with the rhythms of daily existence, beckoned him into a world far removed from the quietude of the elder's campsite. In this stirring microcosm of humanity, Aaron's journey intersected with Lila's—a young woman whose soulful eyes mirrored a well of deep, unspoken stories.

Sitting in the shadow of an old church, Lila seemed almost out of place amidst the marketplace bustle. Her presence was a quiet counterpoint to the raucousness around her. Aaron, drawn by an invisible thread of kinship, approached her, his steps hesitant yet purposeful. In her eyes, he saw reflections of his uncertainties, the same questions that had haunted him since leaving the elder's guidance.

As Aaron approached Lila, the clamor of the streets seemed to dim, as if the world was pausing to honor the gravity of their meeting. He settled beside her, the space between them charged with an unspoken understanding.

"May I?" Aaron gestured toward the ground next to her, his voice gentle.

Lila nodded, her eyes briefly meeting his before returning to gaze at the passersby. "Prego, please."

Aaron sat, observing her profile. There was a grace in her stillness, a story etched in the lines of her face that spoke of wisdom far beyond her years. Her Mediterranean origins were evident in both her beautiful features and her speech.

"I'm Aaron," he began, breaking the silence.

"Lila," she replied, her voice a soft echo in the bustling surroundings.

There was a pause, a delicate balance between wanting to speak and fearing to intrude. Finally, Aaron ventured, "This town...it's a world unto itself, isn't it?"

Lila's lips curved into a faint smile. "Yes, it's a universe of stories, each person a world, each world a story."

Her words, simple yet profound, struck a chord in Aaron. "And what's your story?" he asked, his tone respectful and curious.

Lila turned to face him fully, her eyes reflecting depths of emotion. "It's a story of loss," she began, her voice steady but laced with underlying pain. "I lost my family, not to fate, but to circumstances...circumstances I could neither control nor comprehend at the time."

Aaron's heart constricted at her words. He understood loss, the gaping hole it left in one's life. "I'm sorry," he murmured.

Lila shook her head slightly. "Don't be. It's a part of who I am now. Loss. It teaches you. It's a harsh teacher, but the lessons, they stay with you."

Aaron nodded, feeling a kinship in her words. "It shapes you, doesn't it? Carves out a part of you and leaves something new in its place."

"Exactly," Lila agreed, a glimmer of appreciation in her eyes. "It's like being reborn, in a way. You're not the same person you were. You can't be."

The conversation flowed naturally from there, a meandering river of words and emotions. Lila spoke of her life after the tragedy, the days filled with a numbing void and the nights haunted by what-ifs and if-onlys.

"But I learned to find meaning in it all," she continued. "I started to see the threads of my life weaving into something new, something different. I realized that my loss, as devastating as it was, gave me a perspective that few have. It made me see the fragility of life, the importance of every moment."

Aaron was enraptured by her resilience and how she transformed her suffering into wisdom. It was a transformation he was intimately familiar with, a journey he was still navigating.

In Lila's story, Aaron found echoes of his search for meaning. Her resilience and ability to find wisdom in the depths of despair resonated with the lessons he had learned from the elder. Though different in the details, her journey was similar in essence—a journey from darkness into light, from loss to understanding.

As they talked, the market around them resumed its pace, but for Aaron and Lila, the world had narrowed to just the two of them, their stories intertwining, their souls conversing in the language of shared experiences and mutual understanding.

In the cocoon of their shared space, Aaron and Lila's conversation delved deeper, weaving through past and present pain and healing. With a foreign accent that hinted at her Italian origins, Lila shared more of her story, revealing the roots of her current predicament.

"I came here from Italy after a tragedy," Lila revealed, her voice tinged with nostalgia and sorrow. "I needed a change, a fresh start. But it's been hard, harder than I expected."

Aaron listened intently, noting the slight inflection in her words that hinted her heritage. "What brought you to this town specifically?" he asked.

Lila sighed, her gaze drifting to the bustling street of shops. "I was seeking something...a piece of my family's past. You see, my father was an artist, a creator of beautiful things. Before he passed, he spoke of a masterpiece he had hidden away, something he wanted me to find when I was ready. It was not just a painting or a sculpture, but something more—something that held a piece of his soul."

Her eyes shimmered with unshed tears as she continued. "He never told me where it was, only left clues, riddles wrapped in his art. I've been trying to piece them together to find this hidden masterpiece. But it's like searching for a ghost in a sea of shadows."

Aaron felt a stir of intrigue and empathy. "And you believe this masterpiece is here, in this town?"

Lila nodded. "Yes, the clues led me here. But I've hit a wall. I don't know where to look next. I feel like I'm running out of time. The town is changing; old buildings razed, new ones erected. I'm afraid his elusive gift might be lost forever if I don't find it soon."

Aaron understood her urgency, the fear of losing a precious connection to her past. "I want to help you, Lila," he said with a firm decisiveness. "Maybe together, we can unravel your father's riddles."

Lila's eyes met his, a mix of surprise and gratitude in her gaze. "Why would you help me? You have your life to live, your path to follow."

Aaron smiled, a sense of purpose igniting within him. "Helping you is a part of my journey. Your quest for your father's work. It's more than just a search for lost art. It's about connecting with your past and understanding your father's legacy. And in a way, it mirrors my search for understanding and meaning."

Lila considered his words, the walls around her heart crumbling ever so slightly. "I've been so alone in this," she admitted. "Having someone by my side, someone who understands loss and the search for meaning... would mean more than I can say."

An that moment, a bond was forged between them, a partnership rooted in mutual understanding and a shared mission. Lila's quest to find her father's past became intertwined with Aaron's spiritual journey, each step forward a discovery in both stories.

The noise and bustle of the town faded into a backdrop as they commenced this shared endeavor. Aaron, filled with a renewed sense of purpose, walked beside Lila, ready to help her unravel the mystery of her father's legacy. Their journey together was a new chapter that promised to reveal not just the secrets of a hidden masterpiece but also deeper truths about themselves and the intricacies of the human spirit.

Amidst their conversation, Aaron, recalling a moment from his earlier journey, murmured under his breath, "In sua voluntade è nostra pace." It was a quote from Dante's *Inferno* he had seen inscribed on the pillars of the town's library during his encounter with the old man.

Lila's ears perked up at the Latin phrase. "What did you just say?" she asked, her curiosity piqued.

Aaron repeated, "In sua voluntade è nostra pace—In His will is our peace. I saw it at some old bookstore, inscribed on the entrance."

Lila's eyes sparkled with a sudden realization. "The bookstore!" she exclaimed, impulsively grabbing Aaron and kissing his cheek. "Of course, let's go there. It could be the clue I've been missing!"

This rather serendipitous moment led them to an old bookstore, its shelves laden with dusty tomes and forgotten stories. The owner, his face etched with the lines of countless stories and years of wisdom, gazed intently with eyes that sparkled with alertness and understanding. His posture, though slightly bent by the years, radiated an undeniable sharpness of intellect and a keen awareness of the world around him. Joseph remembered Lila's father. "Ah, yes, the artist. He used to come here, always searching for rare books," he said, his voice a whisper of the past.

Lila's eyes lit up with recognition. "He loved mythology, especially stories about hidden treasures and secret realms. Maybe he left something here."

Together, they scoured the shelves, examining each volume that might hold a clue. Joseph looked on with curiosity and humor; finally, he could not contain himself. "My dear, Dante's *Inferno*. Fourth shelf down, on the left, halfway. Consequently, it was a favor to your father to inscribe the inscription on the entrance. He was a very convincing chap."

In a tattered script of Dante's *Inferno*, they found the first real lead—a small sketch tucked between the pages depicting a pair of descending doves, wings spread wide. Looking on with almost a knowing curiosity, Joseph waved his hand at Aaron and Lila and said, "Off you go now. Adventure and answers await."

As they stepped outside, Lila's gaze was locked onto the picture, her fingers delicately skimming over its surface, following the curves of the doves' wings. "This must signify something," she whispered, absorbed in the sketch. "My father saw meaning in symbols, in the subtle language they spoke."

At her side, Aaron's hand moved instinctively to his forearm, fingers tracing the outline of the tattooed phoenix. Although the imagery of his tattoo differed from the doves, it stirred a similar urge within him—a drive to seek out hidden truths. The winged emblem on his skin, a symbol of change and renewal, seemed to echo the essence of their quest.

"Statues...the cemetery," Aaron voiced, breaking the quiet that had enveloped them.

Lila turned toward him, concern etching her features. "Your arm—is everything alright?"

Aaron's attention shifted, realizing he had been absentmindedly rubbing his tattoo. "It's just the tattoo. It gets itchy at times."

"It's quite beautiful," Lila remarked.

Aaron cast his eyes downward, concealing the deeper pain the phoenix represented. "The cemetery," he reiterated, trying to redirect their focus. "Dove statues are common in cemeteries."

As the hours passed, they pieced together more clues. Their journey took them from the cemetery through the heart of the town and into its forgotten corners. Each location brought them closer to the masterpiece, each discovery a step deeper into the depths of Lila's father's mind.

Four long days were filled with exploration and revelation, nights spent unraveling the complex clues and riddles. The quest became more than just a search for a lost piece of art; it became a journey into the heart of creativity and the enduring bonds of family.

As they delved deeper into the mystery, Aaron and Lila grew closer, their souls intertwined by the shared purpose and the intimate nature of their quest. They shared stories of their pasts, hopes, and fears, their conversation flowing like a river, sometimes calm, sometimes turbulent, but always moving forward.

In a small, secluded garden, hidden behind an old chapel, they found the final clue—a mosaic on the ground, its tiles forming the image of a tree with roots spreading deep into the earth. Lila gasped in recognition. "The Tree of Life...my father's favorite symbol. He said it represented connection, growth, and the eternal cycle of life."

The mosaic's enigmatic message guided Aaron and Lila to an old villa on the town's periphery, a relic from a bygone era, now enshrouded in the embrace of time. The villa, a shadow of its former splendor, a boarding house for traveling aristocrats, was a silent guardian of secrets and legacies.

As they stepped through its weathered doors, a hushed reverence filled the air. The interior was cloaked in dust and memories, whispering tales of days long past. They found their way to the main hall, where the air thickened with anticipation.

Above them, the masterpiece unfolded—a magnificent and alive mural covering the entire ceiling. It was a Tree of Life, depicted with such intricate detail that it seemed to breathe. Its branches stretched upwards, reaching for a sky brimming with stars, each leaf a testament to the artist's love for detail, each star a spark of his profound genius.

Under the celestial canopy, Lila's breath caught in her throat. Tears, unbidden, streamed down her cheeks, carving rivers of raw emotion. "He left this for me," she whispered, her voice trembling with a torrent of wonder, grief, and love. "A piece of his soul, his eternal message— of love, of life's interconnectedness."

Standing beside her, Aaron felt a surge of powerful empathy that was almost palpable. The mural wasn't just art; it was a bridge between hearts, a dialogue between souls separated by the veil of mortality. "He's still with you, Lila," he said softly, his voice barely more than a whisper. "In every brushstroke, in every hue, he speaks to you, through time, through art."

As Aaron and Lila stood beneath the sprawling branches of the painted tree, enveloped in the artist's embrace, the air around them thrummed with a profound sense of completion. The mural was an embodiment of love and legacy. It was more than art. It was a final message from a father to his daughter.

Their moment of reverence was gently interrupted by the soft clicking of a door. Turning, they saw Joseph from the bookstore stepping into the hall. He was holding a set of keys and some paperwork. The air was still as he approached Lila, extending these items to her with a reverence that spoke of deep respect and unspoken stories.

"Your father was more than a friend to me," Joseph's voice was rich with emotion. "He was a confidant, a kindred spirit. He intended to be here, with you, at this moment, to witness the culmination of your quest. But in his absence, he left me the honor of passing on his final gift."

He handed her the deed to the villa and the keys, a tangible symbol of her father's enduring love and presence. "This," he said, his eyes glistening, "is yours now. His legacy, his masterpiece, his final act of love. Your destiny to unfold."

Lila, overwhelmed by the magnitude of the revelation, clasped the deed and keys close to her heart. Her journey had reached its end, but it was an end that marked a new beginning. She had found more than her father's masterpiece; she had uncovered a part of her soul that would forever keep her connected to him.

This moment was a mirror for Aaron, reflecting his journey and the trials he had faced. As he witnessed Lila's closure, a realization dawned upon him. His trial wasn't just about aiding Lila but about understanding the nature of gifts and legacies. The box given to him by the old man under the oak tree was not just an object; it was a vessel of knowledge, a legacy to be unlocked.

His gaze drifted back to the mural, and his eyes caught a series of symbols nestled within the tree branches—symbols mirrored those on the box. In that instant, it all clicked into place. The box was a part of this journey, a larger puzzle connecting him to the stories and legacies of those he met.

Aaron realized that his spiritual takeaway was about understanding the interconnectedness of lives and stories. Each person he encountered, each story he became a part of, was a thread in the fabric of his growth and understanding. The box symbolized this journey, a tangible connection to the wisdom and experiences he had gathered.

With a newfound sense of purpose, Aaron turned to Lila. Their paths had converged for a reason, each aiding the other in finding closure and understanding. Yet, as much as their journey together had changed them, they both knew it was time to part ways to continue their respective paths enriched by the experiences they shared.

With the deed to the villa and the keys in her hands, Lila stood proud, shimmering with her father's love. With the box in his possession, Aaron now understood its significance—it was a key to unlocking the wisdom he had accumulated, a guide to further self-discovery.

As they stepped out of the villa, the first light of dawn breaking over the horizon, their farewell was a silent acknowledgment of their shared journey and the separate paths they must now walk. The mural, the villa, the box—they were all part of a larger mystery of life, love, and legacy. As they walked away from the villa, each carried a piece of this experience in their hearts, a treasure that would continue to guide and inspire them on their respective journeys.

The Symphony of Lives & Living

Beneath a blanket of stars, Aaron returned to the old campsite, where life had once teetered on the edge of oblivion. The elder who had been his savior was absent, yet his essence seemed to permeate the night air, a silent companion in Aaron's solitary reflection.

"Elder, the paths I've walked since we parted are beyond words," Aaron whispered into the stillness, imagining the old man beside him, an attentive listener to the tales of his journey.

His mind first wandered to the encounters that, while profound, had not stirred his soul's deepest waters. These experiences were like gentle breezes in the expansive journey of his life.

In the pulsating core of a city alive with the ceaseless ebb and flow of humanity, Aaron sat across from a Utilitarian philosopher in a lively, bustling café. The aroma of freshly brewed coffee mingled with the spirited buzz of conversation, created an atmosphere ripe for philosophical debate. The philosopher, a man whose sharp features were softened by an ever-present, thoughtful smile, had a way of speaking that was both incisive and inviting, drawing Aaron into a world where every action held profound ethical weight.

Their conversations began with the basic tenets of Utilitarianism, exploring the foundational idea of the greatest happiness principle—the notion that the moral worth of an action is determined by its contribution to overall utility in maximizing happiness or pleasure as summed among all people. The philosopher used everyday examples, from mundane choices like recycling to complex societal issues like healthcare policies, to illustrate how Utilitarianism applied to personal and public domains.

As Aaron absorbed these ideas, he was struck by the practicality of this philosophy. It was a way of thinking that demanded a constant evaluation of one's actions based on the potential to produce the greatest good. The discussions delved deeper, examining historical examples and thought experiments. They pondered the classic 'trolley problem,' where Aaron grappled with the moral dilemma of sacrificing one life to save many, an ethical dilemma he faced too many times in the thralls of combat. Such scenarios, though hypothetical, illuminated the challenging, realistic decisions that leaders and individuals often face.

With a gentle yet persuasive manner, the philosopher guided Aaron through the complex landscape of Utilitarian ethics. They discussed the work of philosophers like Jeremy Bentham and John Stuart Mill, dissecting their theories and contributions to this school of thought. The concept of *utility* was dissected, revealing its multifaceted nature—it wasn't just about simple pleasure but a broader conception of well-being.

One particular afternoon, the conversation turned to the criticisms and limitations of Utilitarianism. The philosopher presented scenarios where following Utilitarian principles could lead to morally questionable outcomes, like justifying the sacrifice of a few for the greater good. This prompted a discussion on the balance between collective welfare and individual rights, pushing Aaron to consider this philosophy's complexities and potential pitfalls.

Throughout these dialogues, Aaron reflected on his own life choices and their impact on those around him. He began to view his journey not just as a personal quest for enlightenment but as a series of decisions that contributed to a larger web of societal welfare. The Utilitarian perspective instilled in him a sense of responsibility toward the collective happiness of humanity, encouraging him to consider the wider consequences of his actions.

As the days turned into weeks, these café meetings with the Utilitarian philosopher became a cornerstone of Aaron's time in the city. Each session gave him new insights and a growing appreciation for the intricate mingle between ethics, personal choice, and the greater good. This chapter in his journey, rich in intellectual stimulation and moral introspection, profoundly shaped his worldview, equipping him with a philosophical toolkit to inform his decisions and actions in the years to come.

Leaving the analytical world of the café behind, Aaron found himself wandering the cobblestone streets of an old town, where history whispered from every nook and cranny. It was here, amidst the rustic charm, that he stumbled upon a small, somewhat eccentric theater. The marquee announced the latest play by a local playwright renowned for her absurdist style. Intrigued, Aaron decided to attend the evening's performance.

The theater was intimate, with an air of unconventional charm. As the lights dimmed, the playwright herself took the stage for a brief introduction. She was a vision of flamboyance, her attire a vibrant clash of colors and patterns, her hair an untamed mane of curls. "Welcome to a journey through the absurd!" she declared with a theatrical flourish, her voice rich with mischief. "Where logic takes a holiday, and reason gets a playful twist!"

The play that unfolded was a whirlwind of bizarre scenarios. Characters found themselves in situations both outlandish and oddly reflective of the human condition.

A man argued fervently with a sentient lamp post over the meaning of light, a woman fell in love with a mirror only to realize she was enamored with her reflection, and a group of philosophers became lost in a forest, debating whether the trees existed if they couldn't philosophically prove it.

After the play, Aaron had the opportunity to speak with the playwright, Isadora. "Your play was...unexpected," quipped Aaron, a wry smile on his face.

"Unexpected is just another word for life, isn't it?" Isadora replied, her eyes twinkling with amusement.

Aaron chuckled. "I suppose so. But isn't there a risk that we might lose sight of reality in embracing the absurd?"

Isadora leaned in, her expression mock-serious. "Ah, but what is reality? If a man speaks in a forest and no woman is around to hear him, is he still wrong?"

Aaron laughed out loud, the sound echoing in the small theater. "So, we're just characters in a play of the absurd?"

"Exactly," Isadora exclaimed. "Life doesn't always make sense, and that's the beauty of it. The world is our stage, and we are the players and portrayers in the limelight, improvising our lines as we go along. We are each other's audience! The key is enjoying the performance and not getting too hung up on the script."

Their conversation continued a delightful dance of wit and wisdom. Isadora spoke of her plays as mirrors to life's unpredictability, tools to challenge perceptions and embrace the chaos with a light heart. Aaron shared his journey, the lessons learned, and the philosophies encountered.

As they parted ways, Aaron felt a lightness in his step, a newfound appreciation for the whimsical side of life. Isadora's perspective, vastly different from the Utilitarian philosophy, had opened a new door for him. It was a reminder that amidst the complexity and confusion of existence, there was always room for humor, for the unexpected, for the joy of the absurd.

This encounter with the flamboyant playwright and her world of absurdity was a vibrant thread in the fabric of Aaron's journey, a splash of color on the canvas of his quest for understanding. It taught him to embrace life's unpredictabilities with a sense of humor and an open heart, preparing him for the deeper philosophical explorations ahead.

In the heart of a bustling town, nestled quietly like a serene oasis, stood the Sikh temple that Aaron stumbled upon. Its architecture was a harmonious blend of grandeur and simplicity, an embodiment of the community's values. The temple's doors stood open, an unspoken invitation to all who sought peace and connection. In this haven of tranquility, Aaron discovered the profound beauty of seva—the selfless service that forms the cornerstone of Sikhism.

Slightly out of breath and suffering from another ear-ringing migraine attack, Aaron stepped into the temple. He was greeted with warm smiles and nods. The air was filled with the gentle hum of hymns and the aroma of spices and herbs, which helped ease his throbbing head.

A gentle touch caressed his shoulder, "Are you alright?" inquired a voice, soft and filled with concern. "My head...I just need a moment," his voice a whisper. Taking a deep inhalation, Aaron closed his eyes. Behind his lids, a kaleidoscope of bright lights danced, and the slight scent of isopropyl caressed his olfaction. As fleeting as a breath of wind the ominous discomfort faded as quickly as it arrived. "I'm okay," he assured, offering a grateful smile to the woman. "Thank you."

He was led to the langar hall, a large, open space where volunteers bustled about, preparing the communal meal. The principle of langar was simple yet profound: a free meal served to all without distinction of religion, caste, gender, economic status, or ethnicity.

Aaron was handed an apron and ushered into the kitchen. He found himself chopping vegetables alongside an aged gentleman who radiated a sense of calm wisdom. "In Sikhism, we believe that serving others is serving God." The man's knife moved rhythmically through a mound of carrots as he continued to explain, "Langar is not just about feeding the body, but also nourishing the soul."

As they worked, Aaron listened to stories of the temple's community work, tales that spoke volumes about the Sikh commitment to equality and social justice. He learned about Guru Nanak, the founder of Sikhism, and his teachings on the importance of selfless service.

It was a philosophy that transcended religious rituals, aiming to foster a sense of unity and oneness among all people.

When the meal was ready, Aaron helped carry large pots of dal and trays of chapatis to the langar hall. He watched as people from all walks of life sat side by side on the floor, a practice that symbolized the breaking down of social barriers and the promotion of equality. As he served the food, Aaron was struck by the diversity of the congregation—businessmen beside beggars, professors beside laborers, all sharing the same meal in the same space as equals.

After the meal, as Aaron sat sipping chai with some of the temple volunteers, he reflected on the impact of this experience. The langar, he realized, was more than a communal meal; it was a powerful act of unity and love. It was a practical application of spiritual principles, embodying the belief that serving humanity was akin to serving the divine.

This encounter left a lasting impression on Aaron. He carried with him not just the teachings of Sikhism but also a profound sense of respect for the power of community and the impact of selfless service. The experience in the Sikh temple added a new dimension to his journey, emphasizing the significance of compassion and empathy in the quest for spiritual enlightenment. It was a lesson that would resonate deeply with him as he continued to explore life's vastness.

Aaron found himself crossing borders and wandering through the remnants of an ancient civilization, its once-majestic structures now but echoes of a glorious past. In this setting of historical contemplation, he met a Platonist philosopher, a man whose presence seemed to blend seamlessly with the timeless ruins around them.

The philosopher, a figure of contemplative serenity, greeted Aaron with a gentle nod. His eyes, reflecting years of introspection, seemed to look beyond the immediate into realms unseen. They sat amidst the crumbling stones, under the vast expanse of the sky, a fitting backdrop for the profound discussions that would unfold.

"American," the man questioned.

Aaron hesitated, trying to place the accent, "Yes. You?"

"Germany. Serge. Nice to meet you," Serge said.

"Aaron," Aaron replied.

"So, what brings you to the Mayan Ruins of the Mexican Yucatan?" Serge waited patiently for the answer as he sipped water from his flask. Aaron thought about it. Why did he come here? Aaron questioned himself. "I came looking to find a long-lost friend. A former teammate. He's gone, I guess," Aaron softly murmured under his breath.

"Well, come for food and spirit," insisted Serge. Aaron and Serge sat at a beachside cabana in Playa Del Carmen, eating local cuisine and looking out over the vast ocean.

Their dialogue began with the foundations of Platonism—the theory of forms. Serge explained how, according to Plato, the physical world is not the true reality but merely a shadow of the true, ideal world. "Think of it this way," he said, picking up a fallen leaf. "This leaf is imperfect, transient, but it is a mere representation of the perfect, eternal form of a leaf that exists in a different realm."

Aaron listened, intrigued by the idea of a world of perfect forms, a constant and unchanging reality that contrasted with the ever-fluctuating physical world he knew. Serge spoke of the allegory of the cave, how humans are like prisoners, only seeing the shadows on the wall and mistaking them for reality. "Our journey," he said, "is like a climb from the cave's darkness into the light of true knowledge."

As they explored these concepts, Aaron questioned the nature of his reality. They discussed the forms of beauty, justice, and goodness, abstract yet somehow more real than their imperfect manifestations in the physical world. The philosopher's words encouraged Aaron to look beyond the surface, to ponder the existence of an unchanging truth beneath the flux of his sensory experiences.

The ruins around them, remnants of a civilization that had once thrived, served as a poignant illustration of Serge's teachings. What once was tangible and solid had crumbled into dust, yet the ideas, the forms that had inspired their creation, remained.

This encounter with Serge, the Platonist philosopher, was not just an intellectual exercise for Aaron but a transformative experience. It challenged him to think deeply about the ideals that guide human life, the eternal truths that exist beyond the physical, and the pursuit of knowledge that leads to true understanding.

Returning from Mexico, although not finding his comrade, Aaron felt as though he had touched something eternal, an unchanging and absolute part of the universe. The experience had expanded his intellectual horizons and deepened his spiritual quest, infusing his journey with a newfound appreciation for the abstract, the eternal, and the true essence of reality.

Aaron's gaze fixed on the embers, and his thoughts ventured deeper. His metaphorical conversation with the elder shifted to the three most profound influences of the past year: Shinto, Nihilism, and Pantheism.

In a most unlikely encounter, Aaron found himself in a grove, where the whispers of towering trees mingled with the wind's gentle caress. Aaron's unlikely journey into the essence of Shinto began. The Shinto priest, an embodiment of tranquility and wisdom, welcomed Aaron into a world where every rock, stream, and leaf was imbued with Kami, the divine spirits. With his deep connection to the natural world, the priest revealed to Aaron the profound relationship between humans and nature, one that was not of dominion but of harmony and respect.

As they walked through the grove, the priest spoke of the Shinto belief in the sacredness of all creation. "Every element of nature," he explained, "houses a spirit, a Kami. These spirits are not gods in the Western sense, but manifestations of the divine energy that flows through the universe." Aaron was captivated by this view of the world, where the boundaries between the spiritual and physical were blurred and a simple rock could be as revered as a majestic mountain. The priest showed him rituals and ceremonies, each an act of respect and honor toward the Kami, each a reminder of the delicate balance and interdependence of all living things.

This experience with Shinto opened Aaron's eyes to a different way of experiencing the world. He found himself more aware of his surroundings, more attuned to the life force present in everything around him. The grove was a sanctuary, a place where he could feel the pulse of the earth and the rhythm of life in its purest form.

However, this serene connection with the natural world was juxtaposed with Aaron's subsequent encounter with Nihilism.

In a smoke-filled café, where the dim lights barely penetrated the haze, a nihilist philosopher challenged Aaron's newfound beliefs. With his piercing gaze and unyielding skepticism, this philosopher presented a very different worldview from the Shinto priest. He spoke of life's inherent meaninglessness, the absence of any divine plan or purpose.

"The universe is indifferent to our existence," the nihilist stated bluntly. "Our search for meaning is a quixotic quest in the face of an uncaring cosmos." These words struck a chord in Aaron, awakening a deep existential dread. The nihilist's perspective was jarring, forcing

Aaron to confront the possibility that the order and purpose he sought might be nothing more than illusions.

Aaron grappled with these ideas—the tranquility he had found in the Shinto grove now overshadowed by a sense of cosmic insignificance. The nihilist's arguments, though bleak, were compelling in their logic. They stripped away the comfort of belief and left Aaron in a landscape of existential uncertainty. This phase of his journey was marked by introspection and doubt as he wrestled with the concept of a universe devoid of inherent meaning.

It was during this existential turmoil that Aaron encountered Pantheism, a philosophy that offered a radically divergent perspective from both Shinto and Nihilism. Pantheism's view of the divine as inherent in all aspects of the universe provided Aaron a new lens through which to view existence. He met a Pantheist sage whose life was a testament to the belief in the unity of all things.

"Everything," the sage explained, "from the smallest grain of sand to the vastest galaxy, is a manifestation of the divine. The divine is not separate from the world; it is the world." This idea resonated with the interconnectedness Aaron had experienced in Shinto, but it also offered a counterpoint to the nihilistic view of a meaningless universe.

Through Pantheism, Aaron began to see the world as arrays of divine expression, each thread a vital part of the whole. This perspective rekindled the sense of

wonder and awe that Nihilism had threatened to extin-
guish. The universe, under the lens of Pantheism, was
alive with meaning and purpose, not because it was be-
stowed from a higher power but because it was inherent
in the very fabric of existence.

As Aaron reflected on these experiences, he realized the intricate interplay between these philosophies.
Shinto had opened his eyes to the divine in nature, Nihilism had challenged him with the abyss of meaninglessness, and Pantheism had offered a vision of a universe
imbued with divinity. Each philosophy had stretched
and molded his understanding in different ways.

The serenity of Shinto had provided a foundation
of harmony and respect for the natural world. Nihilism,
with its stark realism, had forced him to confront the
possibility of a universe without predetermined meaning. And Pantheism had brought him to a realization of
the divine as an intrinsic part of the universe, a force
that connected all things.

These philosophical explorations were not just intellectual exercises; they were transformative experiences
that reshaped Aaron's worldview and his place in the
cosmos. They tested his beliefs, honed his understanding, and ultimately guided him toward a more enlightened and nuanced perception of reality. In the synthesis
of these ideas, Aaron found a profound depth of understanding, a realization that the journey for truth was as
intricate and varied as the universe itself.

The night waned as the fire reduced to a soft glow, casting a gentle light on Aaron's contemplative expression. In the tranquil silence, under the watchful eyes of the stars, he felt a deep sense of gratitude for the paths he had traversed. Each philosophy, each sage, had been an essential step in his ongoing quest for enlightenment, for understanding the vast spectrum of lives and living.

As Aaron nestled into his sleeping bag, watching the final embers of the fire fade into darkness, his eyelids began to droop in the comforting embrace of sleep. But just as he was about to surrender to slumber, he bolted upright, a sudden realization lighting up his face. "Oh, I forgot something important," he murmured, as if the elder were still there listening.

Amid his profound philosophical journeys, there was a practical aspect of his adventures that Aaron had overlooked in his metaphorical conversation. The plane crash that had nearly claimed his life had also serendipitously left him with, still uncounted, millions of dollars. Reflecting on this, Aaron realized how he had unconsciously woven this fortune into the fabric of his journey, using it to extend his impact beyond philosophical contemplation to tangible action.

Throughout his travels, Aaron had discreetly channeled this wealth into acts of kindness and support. He had donated anonymously to charities, aiding causes that resonated with his journey. In places where he had found profound wisdom and solace, he had left behind tokens of his gratitude. He had contributed a generous sum to the Shinto shrine, allowing them to construct a daycare that would serve the community and connect more people to the tranquility he had found there.

He remembered the old theater where the absurdist playwright brought laughter and contemplation into people's lives. With his financial help, the theater underwent renovations and upgrades, transforming it into a modern space that retained its unique character, a sanctuary for the arts, and a beacon for the community.

Aaron had initiated projects in various cities and towns to build shelters for homeless veterans, recognizing the struggles of those who, like him, had served their country. These shelters were more than just a roof and walls; they were places of hope, offering support, counseling, and a chance for a new beginning.

Aaron also thought of Lila, his beautiful Italian friend who had played such a pivotal role in his journey. In her honor, he had anonymously funded the restoration of her historic villa, recapturing its historic aesthetic and grandeur, turning it into a combination of an art museum and a bed-and-breakfast. This place would preserve cultural heritage and provide a space for artists and travelers to find inspiration and rest. Not to mention the preservation of Lila's father's masterpiece.

As Aaron lay enveloped in the serenity of the night, the weight of his recent actions gently pressed upon his consciousness. He recognized that his path had transcended the pursuit of personal awakening; it had morphed into a vessel for dispensing kindness, a tangible force for good. The unexpected boon of his wealth had been transformed into a beacon of positive change, its ripples touching lives in unseen yet profound ways.

With a faint smile gracing his lips, Aaron nestled deeper into his sleeping bag, comforted by the notion that his passage through this world had sowed seeds of goodwill and hope. As the final flicker of the campfire's glow succumbed to the enveloping darkness, a tranquil hush cradled him. His eyes drifted shut, and he slipped away from the tangible world.

As sleep enveloped Aaron, the contours of reality began to blur, ushering him into a realm where visions held a disquieting clarity. There, in the depths of his mind, a scene unfolded with unsettling familiarity. He was adrift in a half-world, a space that was neither entirely dream nor pure reality. It was as if he were walking a tightrope between consciousness and the unknown.

In this eerie interlude, Aaron felt an unnerving sensation of being on the edge, his existence hanging by a thread. The atmosphere around him was tinged with a hospital's sterile, antiseptic smell, not the natural world he so cherished. Heartbeats echoed in his ears. Not in the rhythmic, reassuring thump of life, but in erratic, faltering beats that spoke of fragility and uncertainty.

Glimpses of white-clad figures flitted at the periphery of his vision, their faces obscured, their presence both comforting and ominous. A cold touch, perhaps a hand or a medical instrument, brushed against his skin, sending shivers down his spine. His chest tightened, not with pain, but with the ghost of an ache, a reminder of a vulnerability that was as much mental as it was physical.

In this liminal state, where the boundaries of his journey seemed to dissolve, Aaron's pursuit of wisdom and the warmth of his benevolent acts were momentarily overshadowed. They were replaced by a haunting vulnerability, a silent acknowledgment of the fragile thread that tethered him to life. It was a vivid, almost lucid experience, leaving him with an echo of fear, an unarticulated premonition that lingered at the edge of his waking thoughts.

As the vision receded, like mist dissolving under the morning sun, Aaron's mind gradually steered away from the unsettling precipice of existence. The sterile, ghostly echoes of the hospital faded into the distance, replaced by the gentle cadence of the forest's nocturnal chorus. The imagined cold touch transformed into the soft warmth of his sleeping bag, reassuring him of his presence in the here and now.

The tranquility of the natural world seeped back into his consciousness, wrapping him in a comforting embrace. The rhythmic whisper of the wind through the trees, the distant hoot of an owl, the croaking chorus of toads, and the subtle rustling of nocturnal creatures lulled him deeper into relaxation. His heartbeat, once erratic in his vision, now settled into a steady, soothing rhythm, syncing with the gentle, restorative energies of the earth.

In this serene atmosphere, Aaron's body relaxed, and his mind cleared, releasing the last vestiges of the haunting vision. A sense of peace enveloped him, a soft blanket of calm that promised rest and renewal. With a deep, contented sigh, he surrendered fully to the embrace of sleep, his spirit drifting into a restful, dreamless slumber far from the shadows of fear and uncertainty. This peaceful rest, under the canopy of stars and the watchful eyes of the forest, was a balm to his soul, a reminder of the enduring strength and resilience within him.

The Mirror of Reflection

As the first light of dawn painted the horizon, a new day awaited. It was a promise of another chapter in his unplanned, cross-country pilgrimage. A journey that meandered as much through the landscapes of his inner world as it did across the vast expanse of the country. Amidst the unpredictability of his travels, there was an underlying current of joy and fulfillment.

Aaron had always longed to see the country and immerse himself in its diversity of culture, landscape, and experience. Now, he was living that dream. Each day brought the thrill of discovery, the pleasure of new encounters, and the beauty of unseen vistas. Whether it was the rolling hills that unfolded like emerald waves, the bustling towns with their unique characters and stories, or the serene, starlit nights under the open sky, each moment was a cherished entry in the journal of his soul.

Spontaneous and loosely directed as it was, this journey held a special kind of freedom for Aaron. It was a freedom of movement and spirit—a chance to connect with the essence of life in its purest form. As he traveled, Aaron found joy in the destinations and the journey itself, in the simple act of being and experiencing, unburdened by rigid plans or expectations. Each new sunrise was a canvas of possibilities. Aaron embraced this adventure with an open heart, eager to see where the road would take him next. On this day, a thriving urban expanse caught his attention.

The city's heart throbbed with the relentless rhythm of life. Within its dissonant pulse, Aaron had created a tranquil sanctuary. It was his latest project—a shelter for homeless veterans, a bastion of hope amidst the urban wilderness. As the waning glow of the afternoon sun reflected off steel-glass hi-rises, Aaron's eyes surveyed the fruits of his labor. The shelter, with its freshly painted walls and welcoming aura, mirrored his transformative journey—a symbol of redemption and renewal.

A shadow from his past materialized, piercing the moment's tranquility. Aaron stood, confused, lost in contemplation. Weathered by time and turmoil, a figure approached—a ghost from Aaron's days downrange as a SEAL, a mirror reflecting the person he once was. This man, whose eyes bore the scars of battles unseen and unspoken, was a stark reminder of the path Aaron had once trodden—a path marked by courage and violence, honor and horror.

Their eyes met. And in that locked gaze, a torrent of memories flooded back. Aaron saw himself in this man— the warrior he had been, the soul he had fought to save. This veteran, Brian, who now stood before him in the twilight of his battles, was a living echo of the day that forever altered Aaron's destiny. It was a day etched in the annals of their unit's history—a Day of Valor and loss, where Aaron's heroism had earned him a Purple Heart, but at a cost too steep to bear.

The air between them grew dense, charged with the electricity of unspoken words and unshed tears. Brian's eyes, haunted pools reflecting the agony of a past that clung to him like a shroud, bore into Aaron's soul.

"You," Brian's voice cracked, a blade of accusation, "You were there. You remember, don't you?"

Aaron's throat tightened, the past rising like a tempest within him. "I remember Brian," he whispered, his voice a ghost of its former self.

Brian stepped closer, his presence a storm of raw emotion. "You saved me, not Jake. Why me, Aaron? Why not Jake?"

Aaron's heart pounded, a drum of guilt and confusion. "I...I had to make a choice. It was chaos, I didn't—"

"Choice?!" The word erupted from Brian, a volcano of rage and sorrow. "Jake was more than a brother to me. You chose to let him die!"

Tears brimmed in Brian's eyes, a deluge of pain and loss. "Every night, I see his face, asking me why I wasn't there to save him. Why he had to die alone."

In the oppressive darkness of the desert night, Aaron's SEAL platoon was tasked with a dangerous and urgent mission. Their objective was to rescue members of a Ranger unit, including Brian, who had been captured following an ambush. Time was of the essence to prevent these men from being sold into enemy hands.

As the SEALs embarked on their perilous rescue, they faced fierce resistance. The night air was rent with gunfire, a cacophony of danger and determination. Despite the overwhelming odds, the SEALs pierced the enemy's defenses, showcasing their unyielding resolve and formidable skills.

In the heart of this chaos, Aaron and his teammate breached a building believed to be holding the hostages. Suddenly, they found themselves in the line of fire. A grenade, thrown with deadly intent, erupted in a blast of fire and shrapnel, turning the building into a fatal trap. With no thought for his own safety, Aaron's instincts propelled him into action. He shielded his teammate from the blast's worst, then, with relentless courage, went back into the inferno.

Within, Aaron was confronted with a tormenting scene. Amidst the debris, he found Brian, one of the captured Rangers, under heavy fire. Another grenade arced through the air, its explosive potential clear. Reacting swiftly, Aaron dove toward Brian, pushing them both into scant cover, shielding him from the blast. He then dragged the injured Ranger to safety despite his own body being lacerated by gunfire and shrapnel.

But the building, now consumed by flames, became an insurmountable barrier to further rescue. With a heavy heart and enemy forces closing in, Aaron made the agonizing decision to retreat. Though he saved Brian and a fellow SEAL, his bravery came at a significant cost.

Aaron was awarded a Purple Heart for his valor and selflessness under fire. This honor was a poignant paradox, echoing the mission's ambivalent legacy. It was an ode to bravery birthed in the obscure depths of war, a reflection of sacrifices made within the veil of turmoil.

Aaron felt the weight of the man's grief, a crushing burden. "Brian, I am so sorry," he stammered, his words faltering under the heavy gaze of the man he once called brother-in-arms. "I live with that day every moment. It haunts me, too."

The veteran's face twisted into a mask of anguish and despair. "You got to move on, got to be the hero. What did I get? Nightmares and a hole in my soul where my best friend used to be."

Aaron reached out, "Brian," a tentative gesture of empathy, but the veteran recoiled, a wounded animal lashing out in pain. "Don't touch me! You don't get to be the savior today, not for me."

Their conversation was a battlefield of emotions, raged with anger, regret, and a sense of hopelessness that seemed to permeate the air. Brian's soul was lost in his world of grief and accusation, and Aaron, unbalanced and overwhelmed, struggled to find a bridge over the chasm that separated their shared experiences.

Brian's sudden burst of aggression manifested violently as he pushed Aaron, his fist cutting through the air with a mix of grief and rage. Aaron's instincts kicked in; he deftly parried the swing, attempting to diffuse the escalating situation. But Brian, engulfed in a storm of emotions, was relentless. He tackled Aaron to the ground, a tangle of limbs and turbulent feelings.

As they grappled on the ground, Brian drew a revolver from his sweatshirt. The gun, eerily similar to one Aaron himself owned, was now pressed menacingly against Aaron's temple. Confusion flickered in Aaron's eyes as he noted the familiar design of the revolver. "You left him. In the dirt. Like he was nothing. He deserved better, Aaron. He deserved to live. It should have been you," Brian's voice trembled with a volatile mix of accusation and sorrow.

In that tense moment, Aaron felt an odd sense of detachment. He glanced down, catching a glimpse of his dog tag, the metallic surface reflecting the dim light. The dog tag, a silent witness to countless moments of camaraderie and loss, seemed to pulse with a somber resonance. Its presence, a stark reminder of his journey and survival, brought a surreal clarity to the situation.

"If killing me will help. Pull the trigger," Aaron spoke quietly, surrendering to the moment and accepting whatever outcome it might bring.

Brian's resolve wavered, the gun shaking in his grasp. The intensity of his gaze flickered, and then, as if Aaron's calm acceptance had pierced through his anguish, the revolver slipped from his hand. Brian rolled away, his body wracked with sobs. Quickly, other men intervened, gently pulling Brian back and securing the gun.

Aaron, lying still for a moment longer, watched Brian retreat into the dark hallway, his sobs a haunting echo in the room. He made a subtle gesture, halting a man about to call for help. Aaron understood that some wounds needed space more than immediate intervention.

As the room settled back into a heavy quiet, Aaron remained alone. The imprint of the dog tag against his skin hinted at the complexity of their experiences, the unspoken bonds of brotherhood, and the inescapable shadows of war that lingered long after the battlefield.

The night enveloped Brian in its inky cloak, a backdrop to the storm raging within him. In the solitude of his dimly lit room, memories surged like relentless waves, each crashing against his mind's fragile barricades.

Brian's figure loomed in the shadows. A silhouette marred by the ravages of a war that never left him. His eyes, once vibrant with life, now flickered with the ghosts of a past he could not escape. The images tormented him—not of battlefields, but of faces, the faces of those he had served with, especially Jake. Their expressions were frozen in time, a haunting of choices made and lives forever altered.

Brian's breath came in ragged gasps as the scenes replayed in his mind's theater. He saw the moment, again and again, the decision that split his world into before and after. Jake's laughter, once a resounding echo in the barracks, now sounded like a distant echo in a void, a reminder of a bond severed by fate's cruel hand.

The room felt constrictive as if the walls were inching closer, suffocating him with the weight of his remorse. "It should've been me," he whispered to the darkness, a mantra that had become his constant companion. The guilt clung to him like a second skin, an unyielding force that colored every moment of his existence.

In his hands, the bottle was a temporary reprieve, a false prophet promising forgetfulness. Each sip was a step further away from the pain, yet paradoxically, a step deeper into the abyss that was his guilt and sorrow. The pills, scattered carelessly on the table, beckoned with their seductive promise of oblivion.

As Brian succumbed to their call, his mind drifted to that fatal day, the sounds of battle ringing in his ears. He saw himself frozen in time, making the decision that would haunt his every waking moment. The image of Jake falling was a wound that time had refused to heal.

The alcohol and pills wove their potent spell, and Brian felt himself slipping away from the sharp edges of reality. In this hazy twilight, the pain was dulled, the memories blurred, but the relief was fleeting. The specter of Jake loomed larger, a condemning presence in his drug-induced haze.

Brian's last thoughts, as consciousness slipped away, were not of peace but of a profound sadness, a lament for a life lost and another irreparably broken. The room grew quiet, the only sound the shallow, labored breaths of a soul too weary to fight any longer.

And in that stillness, Brian's struggle ended, his spirit departing the battlefield of his mind, leaving a silence more eloquent than any words could ever be. The night, a silent witness to his unraveling, stretched on, indifferent to the tragedy unfolding within its dark embrace.

Once a beacon of hope and transformation, Aaron's world was now shrouded in a veil of desolation. The room within his own homeless shelter, a place meant to be a sanctuary for lost souls, had become the stage for Brian's tragic exit. Aaron sat there amidst the silent echoes of despair. The walls that had once resonated with the promise of new beginnings now stood as mute witnesses to his inner turmoil.

In his hand, a bottle of bourbon, an artifact from a past he thought he had conquered, became his sole companion. Each sip was a bitter reminder of the fragility of the human spirit, a spirit he had vowed to uplift but had failed to protect in Brian's case. The amber liquid, once a symbol of camaraderie and celebration, now tasted like defeat, its warmth unable to fill the cold void expanding within him.

Guilt washed over him in relentless waves, crashing against the shores of his consciousness. He was haunted by the thought that perhaps, in his quest to heal and transform, he had overlooked the deep, unseen scars of those like Brian, whose battles were fought in the silent theaters of their minds.

Rage simmered within him, a raging inferno against the cruelty of fate that had snatched Brian away. Why had he been spared in the plane crash, only to witness such profound suffering? Why had his path led him to this room, where hope had withered and died?

Sorrow engulfed him, a tangible presence in the room where Brian's journey had ended. Aaron's tears mingled with the bourbon, a fusion of regret and pain. He had dreamt of being a lifeline, yet now he felt adrift in a sea of unanswered questions and unresolved grief.

As the night deepened, Aaron's solitary vigil continued, the bottle slowly emptying, each gulp a futile attempt to drown the memories that besieged him. The room, a microcosm of his internal chaos, was suffused with the ghosts of what could have been—a sanctuary turned mausoleum.

In the quiet room imbued with echoes of sorrow, Aaron found himself face to face with Dr. Cameron Rowe, known affectionately as Cam. The room, a part of the shelter Aaron had poured his heart into, had become a sanctuary for this crucial meeting. Cam, a man whose life had journeyed through the depths of combat with Marine Recon to the realms of deep psychological understanding, carried an air of serene wisdom.

Cam's approach to healing was not merely a profession but a synthesis of his life experiences, melded seamlessly with his extensive knowledge of psychology. His understanding was a harmonious blend of existential and humanistic psychology, which emphasizes the human capacity for self-awareness and the freedom to make choices, and Jungian psychology, which delves into the deeper, often unexplored layers of the psyche, combined with the holistic view of Internal Family Systems. This unique fusion offered a comprehensive lens through which Aaron's journey could be understood and navigated.

"Aaron," Cam began, his voice a calm yet resonant timbre in the room's stillness, "inside you, there's a vast landscape, rich and complex. It's filled with different aspects of yourself, each with its own story, needs, and way of protecting you."

Aaron's eyes, reflecting his inner turmoil, replied, "I feel like I'm being torn apart. There's so much conflict and pain that I don't even know where to begin."

"That's a natural feeling when we first confront the intricate dynamics of our inner world," Cam said gently. "Think of yourself as an orchestra conductor. Each musician is an aspect of your psyche, playing its own tune. Sometimes, the music is harmonious; other times, it's dissonant. Our work is to bring harmony to this orchestra."

Cam, leaning forward with an air of earnest attentiveness, gestured toward the array of notes and diagrams spread out between them. "Aaron, each of these symbols and images represents an archetype within your psyche.

They're like ancient roles played out in your subconscious, influencing your life in ways you might not fully realize."

Aaron, his brows furrowed, looked intently at the diagrams. "You mean, these archetypes are a part of me? Like characters in my own story?"

"Exactly," Cam affirmed. "For instance, consider the Warrior archetype. It's not just a symbol of physical strength or aggression but represents a struggle, a fight for something meaningful. Think of your time in the service and your resilience and courage. That's your Warrior archetype at play."

Aaron nodded slowly, a light of recognition in his eyes. "I've always felt driven. Like I had to fight in combat and life. After the crash, that drive intensified."

Cam smiled gently. "That's your Warrior seeking a cause, a mission. But alongside the Warrior, there's also the Healer in you. This part wants to mend, to care for others. It's what led you to establish this shelter."

"The Healer..." Aaron murmured, reflecting on the numerous times he had extended a helping hand without a second thought.

"And then there's the Shadow," Cam continued, his tone shifting slightly. "It's a vital part of your journey. The Shadow holds aspects of yourself that you might have pushed aside or neglected—feelings of vulnerability, fear, even parts of your identity that didn't align with the soldier's persona."

Aaron's gaze drifted, contemplating this. "I've always known about those parts of me that I had to keep hidden, especially in the military. Doubts, fears...I pushed them down."

Cam leaned in, his voice both encouraging and firm. "Acknowledging your Shadow is not about giving in to these feelings but recognizing them as parts of your whole self. It's in this acknowledgment that true healing begins."

As they explored these concepts, Aaron began to piece together the puzzle of his psyche. He recognized the Warrior's strength and resilience, the Healer's empathy and compassion, and the Shadow's depth and complexity. This understanding illuminated the internal conflicts he had faced, the internal battles between the different aspects of himself.

"For veterans like you, Aaron, this journey of self-discovery is crucial. It's not just about coping with what you've experienced but understanding how these experiences have shaped you," Cam explained.

Aaron's reflection turned inwards, seeing his life's journey through a new lens. "I've been trying to orchestrate a symphony without understanding the music. Or, even knowing there was music!"

"That's a good analogy," Cam agreed. "And now, you're learning not just to understand the music but to compose it yourself. It's about integrating these aspects, harmonizing the Warrior's strength with the Healer's compassion and acknowledging the Shadow's lessons."

As they continued their dialogue, Aaron's understanding deepened. He saw how his drive, his need to help others, and his suppressed fears and doubts were integral to his journey. He began to appreciate the complexity of his inner world and the power of acknowledging and integrating these different parts of himself.

This newfound awareness was not just a revelation but a call to action. Aaron realized that his journey of healing and growth was not just personal but something that could inspire and guide others, especially his fellow veterans, who might be wrestling with their own internal conflicts and seeking a path to harmony and understanding.

In this intimate space with Cam as his guide, Aaron embarked on a profound journey of self-discovery. It was a journey that promised personal healing and the potential to offer hope and insight to others who had walked similar paths.

Cam's explanation of Internal Family Systems opened a new window into Aaron's understanding of his psyche. "Think of your mind like a family, Aaron. Each member, or part, has its unique perspective, its own history and motivations. They interact, sometimes harmoniously, sometimes in conflict, just like any family, or your SEAL platoon if that is easier to understand," Cam explained.

Aaron, intrigued by this perspective, leaned in. "So, in a way, the conflicts I feel..."

"Yes," Cam interjected, "they are like platoon member disagreements. A family quarrel. Your Warrior side, the part honed by discipline and combat, often takes charge, especially under stress. But there's also the healer, who seeks peace and recovery, not just for others, but within yourself. And don't forget the protector, always vigilant, guarding against perceived threats. But, sometimes, this part might overshadow others, like the vulnerable child within you that still needs compassion and understanding."

Aaron's brow furrowed in thought. "I always thought these parts of me were at odds. Like I had to choose one over the other."

"That's a common misconception," Cam replied. "In reality, these parts can learn to coexist, to communicate. It's about finding balance and understanding when and why each part takes over. You can start negotiating with them by doing so, bringing harmony to your internal family."

As their time progressed, Aaron began to delve deeper into the dynamics of his internal SEAL platoon. He learned to identify when his Warrior part dominated, often silencing his more subordinate and vulnerable parts. Aaron recognized his inner healer, the medic who sought to soothe and mend not just physical wounds but emotional ones as well. He also understood his protector part, acknowledging its importance while learning to temper its often-overzealous nature.

"Each part has its wisdom, Aaron," Cam reminded him. "Even the ones that seem to cause you trouble. They all have a role in your psyche. The key is understanding their motivations and learning to lead them, not with force but compassion and respect."

This approach was transformative for Aaron. He began to see his internal conflicts not as battles to be won but as conversations to be had. He learned to listen to his inner parts, to understand the fears and pain, and to respond to each with empathy. He discovered he could guide them toward a common goal by acknowledging and respecting each part.

Through this process, Aaron's perception of his own psyche evolved. He no longer saw himself as fragmented but as a complex, multifaceted individual with a rich internal world. This understanding allowed him to approach his internal conflicts with a new sense of clarity and purpose, like an effective team leader.

He applied this newfound knowledge to his feelings surrounding Brian's passing. He understood that his Warrior part felt a sense of failure, his healer part a profound sadness, and his protector part a deep-seated guilt. By acknowledging these reactions and understanding their roots, Aaron began navigating through his grief with a newfound compassion for himself.

This journey with Cam became a critical turning point in Aaron's life. He not only gained insights into his own psyche but also developed tools that he could use to help others, especially veterans, who were struggling with similar internal conflicts. Aaron's story, enriched by his work with Cam, became a beacon of hope and understanding, showing that even the most profound wounds could be addressed through introspection, empathy, and a willingness to embrace the complexity of the human mind.

As Aaron left the room, a newfound awareness pulsated within him. As he traversed the dimly lit halls of the homeless shelter, each step reflective of his journey toward inner harmony. The ornate box rested in his hand, its intricate carvings imbued with mysteries. The weight of the box felt different now, not just a physical presence but a symbolic one, embodying the journey he had undertaken and the lessons learned along the way.

The shelter, once a mere structure of refuge, now resonated with a deeper meaning. Each face he passed, and each story housed within these walls mirrored parts of his journey. As he walked, his fingers traced the enigmatic patterns on the box, contemplating its significance and the secrets it might unlock.

Then, he crossed paths with Sanchez, another veteran whose life had been a story of service, sacrifice, and subsequent struggle. Sanchez, a man of few words but profound presence, noticed the box in Aaron's hand and paused.

Looking up from a small pile of carpentry tools, his eyes reflecting a life of experience, Sanchez remarked, "That's a unique piece you got there."

Aaron stopped, holding the box out. "It was given to me by someone who helped change my perspective. But I'm still trying to figure out what it means, what it's supposed to teach me."

Sanchez peered closely at the carvings, his gaze lingering on the intricate patterns. "You know. In some cultures, boxes like these are more than just containers. They're symbols of knowledge, of secrets waiting to be unlocked. Each pattern, each line could represent a path, a journey that you need to take."

Aaron's interest was piqued, "A journey?"

"Yes," Sanchez continued, "maybe it's not about opening the box, but understanding what it represents. Your path, your trials, the wisdom you've gained. Sometimes, the journey is more important than the destination."

The words struck a chord in Aaron, aligning seamlessly with his recent revelations. Much like his own psyche, the box was not just an object to be unlocked but a riddle to be understood, a reflection of his intricate journey of self-discovery.

Thanking Sanchez for his insight, Aaron continued toward the exit, the box now a comforting weight in his hand. His mind was a whirlwind of thoughts, each a thread weaving into the fabric of his understanding. As he stepped out into the cool evening air, heading toward his pickup truck, he felt a sense of purpose and clarity.

Aaron stepped out into the cool embrace of the evening, the city lights painting a canvas of serene contemplation. The ornate box, now a symbol of his journey, rested securely beside him as he sat in his truck. His mind, a once-turbulent sea, had found peace in the day's revelations.

Upon reflection, Aaron realized the significance of his encounter with Sanchez. Sanchez wasn't just another veteran; he was one of the dedicated subcontractors working tirelessly on the finishing touches of the shelter. His insight into the box gave Aaron a broader understanding, intertwining his physical and psychological journeys.

Aaron thought about the shelter, a cornerstone of his mission to aid others, now held an even deeper meaning. It was more than a structure; it symbolized the journey, the resilience, and the spirit of those it aimed to serve.

With a sudden inspiration, Aaron jumped out of the truck. He sprinted up the stairs, bursting through the front doors with vibrant energy. He found Sanchez still there, overseeing the final work for the night. Aaron approached him, the weight of his decision evident in his demeanor.

"Sanchez," Aaron began, his voice steady with resolve, "I've been thinking about what you said, the journey, and the lessons we learn along the way. This shelter... it's more than just a building. It's a symbol of hope, of new beginnings."

Sanchez looked up, curiosity etched on his face.

"I want to rename the shelter," Aaron continued, "in honor of someone who embodied the spirit of what we're trying to achieve here. I want to call it *Brian's House*."

Sanchez's expression softened, understanding the depth of Aaron's gesture. "That's a fitting tribute," he said, his voice tinged with respect. "Brian's story, and what he represented, will be a beacon for those who come here seeking refuge and a new start."

Aaron nodded, a sense of purpose anchoring his decision. "*Brian's House* will be a place where hope is reborn, where healing journeys begin. It's a way to honor his memory and the path he walked."

As they stood there amidst the growing quiet of the evening, the shelter was witness to their resolve. *Brian's House* would be more than a name; it would be a legacy, a place where struggles, hopes, and dreams would find a haven.

The Trials of
the Soul

In the quaint town of Harmony, the bed & breakfast was a beacon of memories and warmth, nurtured over time by Lila's tender hands. Here, under the shadow of this serene abode, Aaron found himself grappling with the fragility of life. The news of Lila's accident, falling while attempting to clean her father's masterpiece, had brought him rushing back to a place teeming with shared histories and unspoken bonds.

As Lila lay in a coma, her spirit wandering the spaces between worlds, Aaron felt a profound sense of loss engulf him. He took over the running of the B&B, each task a reminder of Lila's gentle touch. The days were long, filled with the quiet busyness of keeping the establishment alive, a tribute to Lila's enduring spirit. And every moment spare, his place was by Lila's side.

During this time of deep introspection and sorrow, Aaron met Ty, a Buddhist monk from Bhutan, whose presence at the B&B seemed almost serendipitous. Ty, with his deep-set eyes and aura of tranquility, reached out to Aaron, sensing the turmoil within him.

Their conversations, often in the B&B's lush gardens, became a solace for Aaron. Ty spoke of life's impermanence, the Buddhist concept of Anicca, with a gentle yet profound authority. "In the ever-flowing river of life, Aaron, everything is transient. Our pain, our joys, the very breath we take. Attachment to these fleeting moments leads to suffering, Dukkha."

Aaron listened, his heart heavy with grief yet open to understanding. "How does one let go of this attachment, Ty? How do I accept this...this void that threatens to engulf me if Lila...if she doesn't make it?"

Ty's voice was compassionate, "In Buddhism, Aaron, we embrace the nature of suffering and seek to understand its origin. In understanding and accepting life's impermanence, we find the path to Nirvana—a state free from suffering. Your deep pain reflects the attachment to love and connection with Lila. It is natural, and it is okay to feel it. But observe this pain; do not let it define you or your journey."

Aaron absorbed Ty's words, allowing them to resonate with his experiences. They ventured into the core teachings of Buddhism, starting with the Four Noble Truths.

"The First Noble Truth is Dukkha, the acknowledgment of suffering," Ty explained gently. "Your life, marked by the echoes of combat, the loss of friends, and now the uncertainty surrounding Lila, embodies this truth. It's not about perpetual suffering but recognizing its existence in life."

Ty then guided Aaron through the Second Truth, Samudaya. "This truth addresses the cause of suffering," he said. "It lies in our cravings, clinging to things, people, and experiences. Your pain, though a natural response to Lila's situation, is also intensified by your attachment to a desired outcome."

As they explored the Third Noble Truth, Nirodha, Ty's voice was soothing yet profound. "Nirodha offers hope, Aaron. It tells us that suffering can cease by relinquishing these attachments and letting go of desire. This isn't about becoming indifferent, but about finding freedom from the chains of attachment."

The Fourth Truth, Magga, was where Ty spent considerable time. "This truth lays out the path to ending suffering, the Eightfold Path. It's a guide for ethical and mental development, a blueprint for leading a life that balances the spiritual and the mundane."

Ty's words danced like leaves in a gentle breeze as he explained the Eightfold Path, each alighting on a different aspect of Aaron's journey.

"Imagine Right Understanding as the first light of dawn," Ty suggested, "It's the moment of clarity after a long night. For you, Aaron, it's the realization in the aftermath of combat and now, with Lila's predicament.

It's seeing the true nature of things, the impermanence and the interconnectedness of all life."

Aaron nodded, the metaphor striking a chord within.

"Right Intent," Ty continued, "is like setting your compass. Your motives, whether in the heat of battle or in the quiet care of this B&B, set the direction of your journey. It's about aligning your inner compass with values of compassion and harmlessness."

As they delved into Right Speech, Ty likened it to a melody. "Your words, Aaron, can be a harmonious tune or a discordant noise. They have the power to heal or to wound. It's about finding the right notes, the truthful and kind words, that create harmony in your interactions."

Ty then connected Right Action to the steps of a dance. "Each step you take, be it in service of your country or the loving upkeep of Lila's dream, is part of this dance. It's about moving gracefully, ethically, with awareness of the impact of your actions."

"Right Livelihood," Ty said, "is akin to planting a garden. How you earn your living and sustain yourself should not harm the earth or its creatures. Like nurturing this B&B, it's about sowing seeds that bring forth life, not destruction."

Discussing Right Effort, Ty's voice grew more animated. "This is about rowing your boat against the current, Aaron. It's the effort to maintain positive thoughts and actions, especially when the tides of life try to steer you off course. It's a relentless yet rewarding struggle."

Ty then described Right Mindfulness as the art of painting. "Each moment is a brushstroke, creating the picture of your life. Being mindful is to be fully present in each stroke, aware of its color and texture, its place in the bigger picture."

Finally, Ty spoke of Right Concentration with a serene smile. "It's like gazing through a telescope, focusing on a distant star. It's the practice of concentrating your mind, sharpening your focus so that clarity and insight can emerge from the depths of meditation."

Aaron felt as if he was on a journey through a landscape of profound wisdom, each of Ty's metaphors painting a vivid picture of the Eightfold Path and its resonance with his life experiences. The teachings seemed to flutter around him, like leaves in an autumn breeze, each landing softly yet profoundly in his heart.

Ty then returned to the concept of detachment. "In Buddhism, detachment isn't about apathy or emotional disconnect. It's about embracing a conscious release of clinging. It's seeing the world and our experiences as they are, transient and ever-changing, and not letting them control our inner peace."

Aaron felt a shift in his perspective. Ty's teachings on detachment stirred something within him. He reflected on his own life, realizing how his attachment to past traumas and his fear for Lila's wellbeing were both sources of his suffering.

"This detachment," Aaron mused, "is like learning to experience life fully, yet without letting the experiences define or consume me."

"Exactly, Aaron," Ty affirmed with a nod. "It's about being fully present in each moment, embracing joy and sorrow, yet not losing oneself to them. It's about finding a balance, where your inner peace remains undisturbed by the ebb and flow of life's circumstances."

The stars twinkled in the night sky as the evening enveloped them. Aaron felt a sense of clarity emerging. Ty's words had opened a door to a new understanding—a path towards healing, not just for his current grief over Lila but for the deeper wounds he had carried for so long.

One evening, word came that Lila had to be resuscitated multiple times. It was a night of profound despair for Aaron, his heart hanging by a thread of hope. Ty stayed with him, a silent pillar of strength, as Aaron grappled with his darkest fears.

In those hours of shadow, Ty spoke of the Buddha's teachings on death and rebirth. "Life, Aaron, is a continuous cycle of birth, death, and rebirth. This cycle, Samsara, is fueled by our desires and attachments. To understand death is to understand the very nature of life itself."

Aaron's sorrow was palpable, "But Ty, how can I just accept this? The thought of losing Lila..."

Ty responded empathetically, "To accept is not to be unfeeling, Aaron. It is to understand the nature of life and to cherish each moment as it is, impermanent yet invaluable. Your love for Lila and the pain of this moment are all part of your journey toward enlightenment. Embrace it. Learn from it and let it guide you to better understand yourself and the universe."

Aaron found himself in a dual existence as the days seamlessly blended into weeks. On the one hand, he was immersed in the tranquil life of the bed & breakfast; on the other, he was anchored to the rhythmic beeping of the machines that stood vigil beside Lila's bed. In the hushed serenity of her room, Aaron kept a devoted watch; each breath a silent plea for her awakening, each moment an oscillation between hope and despair.

During these extended hours in the quiet room, a sacred space seemed to form around them, where the delicate bond between Aaron and Lila became almost tangible. With subdued whispers, he shared stories with her—tales of their past, his innermost fears, and the enlightening insights he had gleaned on his journey. Sometimes, during these one-sided conversations, Aaron experienced a startling sensation. It was as if their roles reversed, and he found himself in Lila's place, lying in a coma, fighting to wake up. These episodes, fleeting yet vivid, had begun during his frequent hospital visits over the months. They left him puzzled and disoriented, blurring the lines between his reality and a parallel existence where he was the one trapped in unconsciousness.

One such evening, as the sun's final rays cast a golden hue through the window, Ty entered the room.

His presence, typically a soothing balm of calm and wisdom, seemed to carry a different weight this time—an air tinged with the somberness of an impending farewell.

"Aaron," Ty began, his voice tinged with the inevitable goodbye, "the time has come for me to continue my journey. Our paths crossed for a reason, and I hope our discussions have brought you peace and understanding."

Aaron, his eyes weary yet grateful, nodded. "Ty, your teachings and presence have been a light in the darkest time. I can't thank you enough for helping me see through the pain and find peace amidst this turmoil."

Ty smiled, a gentle, knowing smile. "Remember, Aaron, the journey is as much within as without. The lessons of the Eightfold Path, the practice of mindfulness and detachment, are tools you carry within you. Use them to navigate the uncertainties of life."

He placed a comforting hand on Aaron's shoulder. "And remember, Lila's journey is her own. Stay with her. Be her anchor. But, let her find her own way back."

As Ty left, his figure slowly disappearing down the hallway, Aaron felt a bittersweet solitude. He turned his gaze back to Lila, her face serene yet distant. The room, filled with the echoes of their past and the silence of their present, seemed to hold its breath, waiting for a sign, a whisper of what the future held.

The chapter of Ty's teachings might have closed, but the lessons he imparted lingered in the air, in the essence of the B&B, and deeply within Aaron's heart. He realized this was not the end of his journey but a continuation, a path he would walk with Lila by his side, in spirit, if not consciousness.

With the soft glow of the bedside lamp casting shadows on the walls, Aaron gently held Lila's hand. In this quiet, sacred space, he whispered promises of hope and an enduring love awaiting awakening.

In that hushed chamber, accompanied only by the gentle rhythm of Lila's breathing, Aaron discovered a newfound determination. His soul's journey had been laden with trials, leading him to this serene vigil. It was a profound affirmation of the human spirit's relentless endurance.

The Unfolding Path

In the corridors of the Bed & Breakfast, time seemed to drift like autumn leaves in a gentle breeze. Aaron's time was filled caring for the B&B. Daily, he visited Lila, her silent form a constant reminder of life's unpredictability. The questions that haunted him, particularly about Lila's awakening, remained unanswered, floating in the air like uncaught whispers.

As the seasons changed, a new chapter began with Ivy's arrival. A practicing Taoist nurse with a serene aura and insightful demeanor, Ivy brought a sense of calm to the B&B that was both soothing and enigmatic. Aaron first met her in Lila's room, surrounded by the hum of medical equipment and Lila's soft, rhythmic breathing.

Their initial conversations were simple and centered around Lila's care. Over time, however, they blossomed into discussions about life, suffering, and the Taoist way of embracing the world's complexities.

One afternoon while they sat by Lila's bedside, Aaron opened up about his internal struggles. "Ivy, I feel torn. Watching Lila like this, day after day, it's like being anchored to a sinking ship. How does one find peace in this?"

Ivy's words about 'The Way' lingered in the air, a profound echo that resonated deeply within Aaron. Her explanation of Taoism, portraying it as the natural order of things, was not just a philosophy; it was a lens through which the complexities of life could be viewed with clarity and acceptance.

Aaron's mind was a whirlpool of thoughts as he pondered Ivy's teachings. The concept of aligning oneself with the natural flow of life and accepting each moment was intriguing and challenging. It required a shift in perspective, a way of seeing the world not as a series of obstacles but as a stream that one flows with, even when it courses through territories of pain and uncertainty.

"But how does one truly accept something so...so heart-wrenching?" Aaron asked, his voice a mix of curiosity and anguish. The pain of Lila's condition, her lingering in a state between presence and absence, was a heavy burden, one that seemed to defy the very notion of acceptance.

Ivy's response was a gentle illumination in the shadows of Aaron's doubts. "It's about embracing both the light and the dark aspects of life, much like the Yin and

Yang," she explained. This ancient Taoist symbol, representing the duality and interdependence of all things, was a fitting metaphor for Aaron's situation. Just as light cannot exist without darkness, joy cannot be fully appreciated without sorrow.

"This acceptance isn't passive; it's an active engagement with life," Ivy continued. "Recognizing the ever-changing nature of things is key. Your presence here with Lila and dedication to the B&B aren't just responsibilities. They are expressions of Wu Wei, effortless action in harmony with the Tao."

Aaron reflected on this notion of Wu Wei, a term he had heard but never fully grasped. It was an action that perfectly aligned with the natural world. An action that did not fight against the current of life but flowed with it. His caring for Lila and his dedication to the B&B could be seen as manifestations of this principle—not as burdens but as natural expressions of his alignment with 'The Way.'

As he absorbed these teachings, Aaron began to view his situation through a new lens. The Taoist philosophy of embracing life's dualities and flowing with the natural course of events provided a framework for understanding his experiences. The sorrow of Lila's condition. The challenges of maintaining the B&B. They were trials to endure and opportunities to practice this ancient wisdom.

Aaron and Ivy's conversations delved deeper into the heart of Taoist philosophy, each adding depth and understanding to Aaron's evolving perspective.

One day, as they sat in the serene garden of the B&B, Ivy elaborated on the Taoist principle of being like water. "Water, in its essence, is the perfect embodiment of Wu Wei," she explained, her eyes reflecting the pond's calm. "It flows effortlessly, adapting to the earth's contours, yet over time, it possesses the strength to reshape landscapes. It's both yielding and persistent."

Aaron contemplated this analogy, observing the gentle flow of the stream that meandered through the garden. The water's journey was not forced; it moved with a natural grace, conforming to and yet subtly altering its path. In this, he saw a reflection of his own journey—a path that required both surrender and strength, the ability to adapt to life's ever-changing circumstances while maintaining his essence.

"In your journey, be like water, Aaron," Ivy continued. "Embrace life's challenges, not as obstacles, but as pathways that shape and refine you. Your ability to adapt, to flow with the circumstances, is where your true strength lies. This flexibility has a profound power—the power to endure, nourish, and evolve."

These discussions with Ivy opened new vistas in Aaron's understanding of Taoism. He learned about Te, the virtue of moral character that naturally arises from living in harmony with the Tao. "Te is not about imposing one's will," Ivy noted, "but about aligning one's actions with the intrinsic nature of the world, leading to a life of virtue and harmony."

As their dialogues grew richer, Aaron began to internalize these principles, applying them to his daily life. How he managed the B&B, his interactions with guests, and his unwavering care for Lila, all began to reflect his understanding of Wu Wei and Te. He found himself moving through his days with a newfound ease, a sense of being in tune with the rhythm of life.

This shift in Aaron's approach was subtle yet profound. In his interactions, there was a gentleness, a patience that stemmed from his deepening grasp of Taoist teachings. He began to see challenges not as burdens but as opportunities to practice the art of Wu Wei, to be like water—resilient yet yielding, strong yet gentle.

Through Ivy's guidance, the principles of Taoism were no longer abstract concepts to Aaron; they were becoming part of his character. Each day, as he navigated the complexities of life at the B&B and the emotional landscape of Lila's prolonged coma, he did so with inner tranquility and outer flexibility, embodying the Taoist way of being in harmony with life's ebb and flow.

As the days stretched into weeks, Aaron's transformation was evident in his demeanor, actions, and outlook. The teachings of Taoism, imparted through Ivy's wisdom, were not just shaping his understanding of the world; they were reshaping him, guiding him towards a path of peace, acceptance, and fluid strength.

One pivotal evening, their conversation took a turn when Ivy shared her challenges. "I've been struggling to reconcile my path with my duties here," she confessed. "There's a part of me that yearns to explore the world, to expand my understanding of Taoism through travel and experience."

Aaron saw a reflection of his own restlessness in Ivy's words. "Maybe, in helping each other, we find our way," he suggested, an idea taking root in his mind. "Perhaps my next step in embracing Taoism is to assist you in pursuing your journey."

This exchange was a turning point for Aaron. In helping Ivy, he saw an opportunity to put into practice the principles of Taoism he had learned — the idea of Wu Wei, of acting in harmony with the natural flow of life, and of the interconnectedness of all beings.

With no sign of Lila awakening, Aaron decided to leave Harmony. It was a choice fueled by his newfound understanding of Taoism and his desire to fund Ivy in her journey. This selfless act of embracing the path presented was his ultimate practice of Taoist teachings.

As Aaron prepared to leave, he stood by Lila's bedside, myriad emotions swirling within him. "Lila, I carry you in my heart," he whispered, "and though I leave, my love remains. This isn't goodbye, but a new beginning."

Leaving the B&B, Aaron felt a mixture of sorrow and hope. He was stepping into the unknown, propelled by a philosophy that had given him a new lens through which to view the world.

The Silent Guide

Far from the echoes of civilization, deep within the embrace of nature, Aaron found himself on a journey of a different kind. The trail he chose, winding through dense forests and over towering peaks, was a path less traveled that demanded resilience and introspection. With no phone or communication with the outside world, Aaron sought the silence his soul yearned.

Aaron ventured into the embrace of the wilderness, each step on the trail a step deeper into the tranquility he sought. The forests he traversed were a mosaic of vibrant greens, the trees standing tall and majestic, their leaves whispering secrets of the ages. Sunlight filtered through the canopy in golden shafts, creating patterns of light and shadow that danced on the forest floor.

The air was fresh and crisp, scented with pine and the earthy aroma of damp soil. As he hiked, the soft rustle of leaves underfoot mingled with the distant calls of birds, creating a natural melody that soothed his spirit. The deeper he went, the more the forest seemed to envelop him, its embrace both comforting and awe-inspiring.

Climbing higher, the dense forest gave way to rugged mountain terrain. The ground beneath his feet became rocky and uneven, challenging his every step. Here, the air was thinner, cooler, with the scent of mountain heather and wild thyme. The vistas opened, revealing panoramic views of rolling hills and distant peaks, their tops shrouded in mist.

Streams meandered through the landscape, their waters clear and cold, gurgling over rocks and pebbles, a refreshing sound that was a constant companion on his journey. Aaron often paused to drink from these natural springs, the water tasting pure and invigorating.

At night, the forest and mountains transformed. The absence of artificial light revealed a sky awash with stars, their brilliance undimmed by human presence. The Milky Way stretched across the heavens, a celestial river amidst the ocean of the universe. The only light was the soft glow of his campfire, its crackling flames casting a warm, comforting glow.

The wilderness was not just a backdrop for Aaron's journey; it was a participant. The rustling leaves, the chirping of crickets at night, and the howling of a distant wolf all spoke to him in a language beyond words. The fragrance of the woods after a rain, the cool touch of morning mist, the rugged feel of bark beneath his hands

—every sense was engaged, drawing him deeper into the moment, into the silence he sought.

Aaron's connection with nature had grown profound. The wilderness was no longer just a place; it had become a part of him, a silent guide on his journey to inner peace. Six weeks into his through-hike, he discovered a picturesque campsite nestled in a valley between several towering mountains beside a tranquil pond. The beauty of the site, with its serene waters reflecting the grandeur of the sky, beckoned him to stay. Time seemed to lose its grip in this hidden haven, days melding into nights with a natural, unspoken rhythm.

One evening, the scent of campfire wafted through the air, an unexpected aroma as Aaron hadn't seen another soul for weeks. His curiosity piqued. The next day, he ventured out, foraging for blueberries and answers. It was then he encountered Tomas.

Tomas was an enigmatic figure with eyes that spoke volumes. He communicated not with words but through actions and expressions. His presence was both a mystery and a revelation. With Tomas, Aaron ventured deeper into the wilderness of the mind, each step an unspoken lesson in the art of listening—to the wind, the rustle of leaves, the distant call of an eagle.

Aaron's days with Tomas unfolded like a dance with nature, each step a lesson in harmony and awareness. Together, they moved through the wilderness with a purposeful ease, attuned to the rhythm of the land.

Their foraging was an exercise in mindfulness. Tomas showed Aaron how to identify edible plants and berries, their hands gently sifting through leaves and soil. He learned to recognize the subtle differences in foliage, the nuances of color and shape that signified nourishment. Foraging became more than just a search for food; it was a way to connect deeply with the earth and understand and appreciate its bounty.

As they navigated the rugged terrain, Tomas's silent guidance was as instructive as any spoken word. He led by example, his steps deliberate yet effortless, finding paths through dense underbrush or across rocky out-crops with an innate sense of direction. Aaron followed, his footsteps becoming more assured as he learned to read the land and see the trail with his eyes and instincts.

The natural world around them was a constant source of wonder and learning. Tomas pointed out the tracks of animals, interpreting their patterns to reveal the stories of their travels. They watched the skies, reading the movements of birds and the shifting of clouds to foretell the weather. Even the wind had its language, whispering through the trees, carrying messages of what lie ahead.

The sky became their canvas as Aaron and Tomas sat by the evening's campfire. Tomas taught Aaron to iden-tify constellations and to navigate by the stars. The night sky was a map of ancient knowledge, each star a point of wisdom. In the silence, with the heavens stretched above them, Aaron felt a profound connection to the universe, a sense of being part of something infinitely more significant than himself.

In this silent companionship, every day was a revelation. Aaron was learning not just to survive in the wilderness but to thrive, to find a sense of peace and purpose in the simplicity of existence. Through his wordless teachings, Tomas showed Aaron how to truly listen to the natural world and to himself. In the silence—in the dance of their daily routines—Aaron found a profound sense of presence, a deepening of his connection to the world and his inner landscape.

Aaron discovered the value of introspection. Away from the noise of human interaction, he found a profound connection with his inner voice. The natural world around him seemed to speak a language understood not by the mind but by the essence of the human soul.

One early morning, amidst the verdant embrace of the forest, Tomas led Aaron to a clearing where the ground was speckled with an array of peculiar white mushrooms. These fungi, Tomas indicated through his actions, were not ordinary; they were sacred, a natural key to unlocking deeper realms of consciousness.

With a reverence that spoke of years of understanding and respect, Tomas carefully harvested a few of these mushrooms. Back at the campsite, Tomas, with the focused mannerisms of a holy man, delicately arranged the sacred fungi upon rocks, facing the sun.

That evening, under a sky awash with stars, they sat together in a circle of stones, the air thick with the anticipation of a journey beyond the physical world. A silent ceremony unfolded as they reverently consumed the mushrooms, ingesting each dried stem and cap. As nature's medicine took hold, a profound sense of connection enveloped Aaron. The boundaries between himself and the world around him began to blur, dissolving into a amalgamated fluidity of sensations and emotions. The forest came alive in ways he had never imagined. Every leaf, every whisper of the wind, felt like a direct communication from the earth.

The experience was reminiscent of his time with the life-saving elder. It was a journey through the essence of the human soul, guided by the silent wisdom of Tomas and the nurturing spirit of nature. Aaron's senses were heightened to an extraordinary degree, allowing him to perceive the world in a spectrum of colors, sounds, and feelings that were previously unknown.

In this altered state, the forest transformed. Trees seemed to breathe with a life of their own, their leaves whispering ancient truths. The stars above appeared closer, as if he could reach out and touch their luminescent trails. The night air was a symphony of scents, each inhalation bringing a new layer of understanding.

As the effects of the mushrooms deepened, Aaron's sense of self began to dissolve, replaced by an overwhelming feeling of oneness with the universe. It was a familiar but forgotten feeling. Similar to the sacred elixirs of the elder, these mushrooms enabled the melting away of fears, doubts, and the barriers he had built around his heart, revealing a raw, unfiltered connection to the world around him.

This journey through the psychedelic realm was a revisited and revised revelation. Aaron encountered his innermost fears, faced them head-on, and emerged with a newfound strength and understanding. He saw his hopes and dreams not as distant desires but as integral parts of his being, waiting to be realized.

In these moments of heightened consciousness, Aaron understood the interconnectedness of all life. He saw himself not as a separate entity but as a part of a grand, universal symphony. Each creature, plant, and element of nature played its part in this symphony, creating a harmonious melody that spoke of the unity of existence.

As the experience gradually subsided, leaving Aaron in a state of awe and tranquility, he realized that these psychedelic journeys were not mere escapades into the unknown. They were profound teachings and experiences connecting him to the deepest truths of the universe and his own soul.

Aaron reflected on these experiences, each memory a treasure trove of wisdom and insight. He began to see the world with new eyes, appreciating the beauty and complexity of life in a way he had.

As days seamlessly unfolded into months, Aaron's journey with Tomas became a spiritual quest. The silent guide, with his mystical teachings and the wise use of psychedelics, had opened the door to a world where silence spoke louder than words, where introspection revealed universal truths.

Ultimately, Aaron understood that the greatest guide was often found within. The silence of the wilderness, the guidance of Tomas, and the mystical experiences had all been conduits to a deeper understanding of himself and the world around him.

The trail drew to an end, and Aaron emerged from the wilderness transformed. He carried with him the lessons of the silent guide—the value of introspection, the wisdom found in silence, and the profound connection with the natural world and the universal everything.

The trail had been more than a physical journey; it had been a pilgrimage of the soul, a silent voyage into the heart of mysticism and the mysteries of existence.

The Convergence of Paths

Aaron's journey now found him behind the wheel of his truck, the landscape outside morphing with each mile. His time with Tomas, the silent guide, lingered in his thoughts, a meditative experience that had woven silence and understanding into a profound personal transformation. The ways he had helped Tomas, though unspoken, were acts of deep empathy—sharing meals, assisting with navigation, and a silent companionship that transcended words. And, although Aaron longed to do more, he understood that Tomas was a solo traveler, a minimalist who wanted nor needed anything. The memory of companionship will be the gift given.

Driving without a specific destination, Aaron reflected on his journey. It was becoming clear that his quest was as much about internal discovery as it was about seeking external wisdom. Each encounter and trial had subtly shaped him, guiding him toward a deeper understanding of his authentic self.

As the road unfolded, Aaron's path crossed with a stranded couple, Anika and Rohan, whose car had broken down. Feeling a natural urge to assist, he offered them a ride. The couple expressed their gratitude for his kindness.

As the truck wove through the tranquil countryside, the conversation became a fluid exchange of philosophies, each thought seamlessly leading into the next. Anika, her voice soft and gentle, wove Hindu wisdom into the fabric of their dialogue, connecting it to Aaron's journey.

"Ganesha, who you embody in overcoming your challenges, teaches us about the power of resilience and the importance of perseverance on our path," Anika said thoughtfully. "Your ability to face and overcome obstacles, much like your experiences in the military and the trials with the plane crash, Brian and Lila, is a dance with Ganesha's energy."

Aaron nodded, introspectively connecting his past hurdles to the deity's symbolism. He recalled how each obstacle had been a gateway, leading him to new insights and growth.

Anika continued, "And Lakshmi's abundance isn't just in material forms. It's in the richness of your journey— the wisdom from the Indian elder, the connection with Lila, the wisdom imparted to you by so many guides.

Each step has been laden with spiritual wealth, an unseen prosperity that Lakshmi symbolizes."

The mention of the elder, the veteran shelters, and especially Lila brought a sense of deep gratitude to Aaron. Indeed, his journey had been rich, not only in material terms, but in invaluable experiences and insights.

Rohan, picking up the thread, seamlessly connected this to existentialist thought. "This richness of experience aligns with existentialism's emphasis on personal journey and authenticity. Dostoevsky's characters often confront profound moral dilemmas, much like your own confrontations with personal demons and moral choices in and after the military. It's in these confrontations that we find our true selves, as Nietzsche suggests in 'becoming who you are.'"

The conversation flowed naturally, with Rohan and Anika's words interlacing the teachings of Hinduism with existentialist wisdom, mirroring Aaron's journey. Aaron realized how his path had reflected these philosophies. This personal argosy was a part of a universal narrative and a unique, self-determined journey.

Anika smiled, adding, "Krishna's wisdom in the Bhagavad Gita about duty and purpose resonates with your path. It's about embracing one's Dharma, one's true role in the cosmic order, just as you've been doing, Aaron. Your experiences, service, generous helping, and quest for healing and understanding are all part of fulfilling your duty to yourself and the world."

Rohan's voice, rich with understanding, added, "And William James's concept of truth's individual essence – it's akin to a Jackson Pollock within your life experiences. Each drip and splatter of paint, from your military service to your healing journey, merges into an abstract expression of your personal truth, reflecting the chaotic yet purposeful nature of existence."

Aaron felt a deepening understanding of his journey as the conversation wove through these philosophical landscapes. The Hindu deities' symbolism mirrored his life's journey, entwined with the existentialist emphasis on individual meaning and authenticity. Each experience, each guide encountered, had contributed to his personal growth, propelling him toward fulfilling his larger role in the universe.

The drive to Anika and Rohan's home became a journey through the confluence of ideas, a harmony of thoughts that resonated deeply with Aaron's experiences. As they arrived, Aaron felt a sense of convergence – his past experiences, the wisdom gained, and the people he had helped, all intricately blended into the richness of life and learning.

In the embrace of their home, surrounded by the symbols of Hinduism and existential thought, Aaron's realizations crystallized. His quest was a coalescence of many paths and had been a journey not just outward into the world but inward into the depths of his soul. This was not an end but a milestone in his journey of self-discovery and understanding.

Aaron found a moment of clarity in the tranquility of their home, surrounded by symbols of both philosophies. His path was not merely a series of random encounters but a deliberate pilgrimage of self-discovery, where each guide and experience served as a stepping-stone towards a deeper understanding of himself and the universe. This realization was a significant milestone in his transformation, a synergy of paths leading to a personal awakening.

Aaron understood what he now must do...

The Awakening

Leaving Anika and Rohan's haven of wisdom, Aaron drove with purpose, each mile bringing him closer to the origin of his transformative journey. His hands lightly grasped the steering wheel, his mind inundated with countless realizations from the night before. The opulent box, now a constant companion in his pocket, felt heavier with meaning after Anika's revelation about destiny and unity.

As he neared the familiar terrain of the desert, the landscape seemed to echo his internal changes. The once intimidating vastness now seemed like a warm embrace, reflecting his transformation from a Navy SEAL Chief to the enlightened soul he was evolving into.

Pulling up to the riverbank where his life had once teetered on the brink, Aaron saw the elder seated by a campfire as if expecting him. The elder's eyes, reflecting the flames, met Aaron's. In that gaze, Aaron felt the final pieces of his journey align.

"Ah, the circle is complete," the elder spoke with a timbre that resonated in Aaron's soul. "Now we must erase it so there are no boundaries or borders."

Sitting across from the elder, the fire crackling between them, Aaron felt a penetrating peace. The elder's sister joined them, her presence adding to the sacredness of the moment. As she smiled at him, he sensed a familiarity in her deep brown eyes.

"The journey you have undertaken," the elder began, "is of the heart. The mind. The soul. You have learned from many, but the greatest lessons lie within you."

Aaron listened, his heart open and mind clear. "I've come to realize," he confessed, "that the answers I've been seeking were always within me. My experiences were all mirrors reflecting what I needed to see in myself."

The elder nodded, "Yes, you have been both the seeker and the sought. Like the Zuñi prayer song, you have been the earth's mother, replete with living waters, nurturing the corn to new beings. You are both the creator and the creation."

His sister remarked, "Your journey reflects our deep connection with the earth, the cosmos, and one another. Lakota wisdom teaches us that harming any part of the Earth, or any being, is harming ourselves. You've learned to live in harmony, not just with nature, but with your authentic self."

As the night deepened, they spoke of existential truths, of the personal nature of reality that William James professed. Aaron shared his experiences, each a stepping-stone on his path to awakening.

"It's like Nietzsche said, 'He who has a why to live can bear almost any how,'" Aaron reflected. "My trials, from the military to the present, have been about finding that 'why,' my purpose."

"And in doing so," the elder added, "you have embraced your Dharma, your duty in the cosmic order, as Krishna taught. You have become, in essence, a warrior of the spirit."

Sitting there, under the vast desert sky, Aaron felt an intense awakening. The culmination of his journey was not just about external wisdom but an inner enlightenment, a realization of his inner authenticity.

As dawn approached, marking the end of their night-long dialogue, Aaron stood up, a changed man. He looked at the elder and his sister, gratitude filling his heart.

In the tranquility of that moment, Aaron felt a significant shift. "I am ready now," he declared, with a resonating sense of determined purpose.

As he stood, ready to embrace his new path, the elder spoke, "There is one more step." His sister, chanting softly in the background, stopped and nodded affirmatively. The elder produced an ancient peace pipe, and as he lit it, he urged Aaron, "Breathe deeply until the nectar of life fills your lungs."

As Aaron drew a deep breath, the world around him began to waver, its edges dissolving into an indistinct haze. Like a whisper from another realm, a peculiar sensation brushed against the fringes of his consciousness. Suddenly, a resonant buzzing filled his ears, a sound that seemed to emanate from the very core of his being. It swelled into a massive headache, a relentless pressure that felt as though it sought to cleave his mind in two.

His chest tightened, gripped by a searing pain that ebbed and flowed with each labored heartbeat. The experience was visceral, alarmingly tangible. Confusion and fear threatened to overwhelm him, yet amidst this turmoil, a fragment of understanding flickered to life. With all the strange encounters and mystifying experiences he had weathered, Aaron knew he had to surrender to this moment, to embrace the uncertainty and face whatever truth it might reveal.

In a state of hyper-awareness, Aaron turned his gaze towards the elder, his eyes a silent plea for enlightenment. The elder met his look with a knowing smile, an expression that seemed to transcend the ordinary confines of wisdom. Then, as sudden as it was unexpected, the elder stood, raised his hand, and delivered a sharp slap to Aaron's forehead. "Wake up!" he commanded, his voice echoing between death and waking, fear and understanding.

Aaron awoke with a jolt, his lungs screaming for air as a blinding white light assaulted his senses. Panic clawed at his chest, his heart pounding like a drum in the echoing void of his mind. The sterility of the room, washed in an unforgiving white, contrasted with the vibrant hues of his recent experiences. The air was heavy with the pungent mix of bleach and alcohol, each breath reminiscent of a reality he couldn't place.

His body felt foreign as if trapped in a shell that didn't belong to him. The sounds around him—the persistent beeping of machines, the distant murmurs of voices—were disjointed, creating a symphony of confusion. He tried to move, but his limbs were leaden, unresponsive to his frantic commands.

A nurse leaned over him, her face a blurred mask of concern. As she gently removed the intubation tube, a raw, scraping sensation ignited in his throat, triggering a cough that rattled his whole body. "You're in the hospital. Calm down, you're okay," she whispered, her voice a soothing balm amidst the chaos of his awakening. "Welcome back."

But welcome back to what? Aaron's thoughts were a whirlwind, a tumultuous sea of images and emotions colliding with the harsh reality of the hospital room. He clutched at the fragments of memory—the elder, the fire, the profound conversations—trying to anchor himself in their fading warmth.

The nurse, her movements precise and practiced, watched him with an expression of awe and disbelief. "Never seen anything like this. I'm not sure how you survived," she murmured more to herself than to him.

Though intended as reassurance, her words only deepened the chasm of his disorientation.

Fear and confusion coursed through Aaron, tangling with the remnants of fading illusory reality. Was it all just a figment of his comatose mind? How could the vividness of his experiences and the depth of his transformations not be real? Yet here he was, in a sterile hospital room, so different from the richness of his journey.

As he lay there, struggling to put together the pieces of his shattered reality, Aaron felt a profound sense of loss. The elder's wisdom, the silent guidance of Tomas, the insightful dialogues with Anika and Rohan—were they merely illusions birthed from the depths of his unconscious mind?

Aaron grappled with the blurred lines between unconscious perceptions and objective reality in this maelstrom of uncertainty. The journey that had reshaped his soul and awakened him to new truths now seemed like a distant echo, leaving him to question his existence.

With its clinical detachment, the room was a cold reminder of his isolation. The scents. The sounds and the sterile atmosphere anchored him in a reality he couldn't reconcile with the spiritual crusade he had just lived. Aaron stood at the crossroads of his consciousness, teetering between two worlds, each vying for his belief and acceptance.

A doctor entered, a look of mild astonishment on his face. "The miracle man has awakened," he declared, echoing the nurse's sentiment.

Aaron took time to process his surroundings, each detail of the room evoking fragments of his inner journey—the TV in the corner, set to a channel playing documentaries on philosophy and mysteries of the world; the nurse, Ivy, reminiscent of the guide from his journey; even the doctor, named Cam, seemed to parallel a figure from his transformative experiences.

The doctor, a man with a demeanor that balanced professional curiosity with genuine concern, took a moment to explain the extraordinary circumstances of Aaron's survival. "It really is the weirdest thing," he began, his tone laced with a mix of disbelief and wonder. "A miracle, really."

Struggling to reconcile his vivid journey and his current reality, Aaron listened intently.

"You didn't just survive the crash," the doctor continued, "you somehow managed to tumble down a mountain, off a cliff, and landed in a mostly dry riverbed. But the odd part—when the rescue team found you, you were surrounded by a community of big toads. They were everywhere—near, around, even on you."

The mention of the toads stirred something within Aaron, a fleeting shadow of a memory, elusive yet familiar. The doctor seemed puzzled by it, too, as if trying to make sense of how these creatures fit into the bizarreness of Aaron's survival.

"These weren't just any toads," the doctor added, a hint of curiosity in his voice. "They were unusually large, and the rescue team said they'd never seen so many in one place before. It's as if they were...watching over you."

Aaron felt a strange connection to this detail, a silent echo of his experiences with the elder and the awakenings he had encountered. The toads, with their hushed, enigmatic presence at the scene of his accident, added another layer of mystery to his already miraculous survival.

The doctor's words lingered in the air. Aaron's ordeal was of an extraordinary and inexplicable nature. The presence of the toads, though unexplained, hinted at something deeper, a subtle nod to the transformative experiences Aaron had undergone in his death-defying metamorphosis.

As the doctor left, Aaron lay in contemplation, the image of the toads at the riverbed intertwining with his memories of the journey. The ambiguity of it all—the surreal illusions, the crash, the toads—left him in a state of wonder, questioning the boundaries between reality and the mystical realms he had traversed.

This silent reference to the toads, potentially a symbol of change and awakening, was a puzzle piece that fit perfectly into the strange nature of his entire experience. Whether a mere coincidence or a meaningful sign, it added to the depth and mystery of Aaron's incredible story of survival and transformation.

As Aaron grappled with the overwhelming sensations, something in the periphery of his vision caught his attention. He glanced upward and noticed his dog tag hanging on the bedpost. The metallic emblem, a silent sentinel of his past and present, seemed to call out to him. Gingerly, he reached for it, each movement laced with a sharp twinge of pain.

His arm, still tender and healing from recent burns, throbbed and itched under the strain. Despite the discomfort, Aaron was drawn to the dog tag, compelled by its familiar weight and the memories it held. He held it up, the light catching the engraved letters—A. R. Gossy. A smile crept across his face, a simple gesture that spoke volumes of the acceptance and acknowledgment of his journey.

Intriguingly, amidst the scorched and healing skin, his phoenix tattoo had endured, its vibrant design largely unscathed. The resilience of the inked bird, rising from the ashes, mirrored Aaron's journey of recovery and transformation, a poignant reminder of endurance amidst adversity.

Over the next few months of brutal but rapid recovery, Aaron recounted his experience to psychologists, doctors, and reporters. Each narrative reflected the notion of him being the *Miracle Man,* a survivor of a catastrophic plane crash from 32,000 feet. The discussions revealed the depth and vividness of his dream, blurring the lines between objective and subjective reality.

On the day of his discharge, Ivy brought Aaron his belongings. She handed him the ornate box and said, "When the rescue team found you, you had this clutched tightly in your hand. It's a miracle it survived the crash like you did." The existence of the box was a tangible connection to another reality, a bridge between two worlds.

Ivy inquired whether she could contact anyone for him. Aaron shook his head. His past, with deceased parents, a long-gone ex-wife, and a solitary life, loomed in his mind. "I just need to be alone, to process—he whispered. As Ivy turned to leave the room, Aaron muttered, "Taoist?" Ivy's bewildered look gave it away. "Wow, yes I am. My father is a Daoshi, although I'm really not seriously into it, I do follow The Way."

Ivy smiled and handed Aaron the keys to his Bronco. This was a friendly gesture from the Navy and his "Team Guy" friends. They had delivered it to the hospital some time ago. Aaron thanked her, stepping into a world that felt familiar yet transformed.

As he drove away from the hospital, the realization dawned on him. Whatever had happened to him, the experience had changed him. The insights, the transformation he underwent, were as real as the desert sun and the ornate box beside him. He was not just Aaron Robert Gossy, the survivor; he was a man reborn, awakened to a new understanding of life. His journey was not over; it was merely taking a new direction.

The Final Journey

Aaron drove aimlessly through the picturesque western mountains of Colorado, his Ford Bronco a vessel for his wandering thoughts. His destination was unclear, Minneapolis, perhaps, but nothing awaited him there anymore. Memories of the crash in the UTE Mountain Reservation and his miraculous recovery in an Albuquerque hospital haunted him, a surreal backdrop to his current reality.

He found himself in a quaint town nestled among the mountains. A place where time seemed to stand still. He spent days there, lost in contemplation, a lone figure grappling with the threads of his past, present, and future.

One morning, in a small diner, Aaron lingered over his coffee, the ornate box by his side. A waitress, her eyes drawn to the box, approached him. "That's quite a conundrum you have there," she commented casually.

"It's more than that," Aaron replied, a hint of melancholy in his voice.

"My grandmother had something very similar when I was younger," and with a gentle, "may I?" she reached for the box. To Aaron's astonishment, she opened it effortlessly, peering inside with a knowing smile. Handing it back to him, Aaron looked inside. He found an old photograph—a younger version of himself with a little girl in a place he recognized from his childhood in the Dolomites.

His heart raced as he turned the photo over. 'Lila and Aaron. Forever.' The words struck him like lightning, igniting a storm of emotions.

He stood up abruptly, a whirlwind of confusion and excitement. "Do you know of a town named Harmony?" he asked urgently.

"There's a Harmony in Colorado, but I'm not sure," she replied with piqued curiosity.

Frantically searching the web, Aaron found nearly thirty towns named Harmony scattered across the United States. A daunting quest loomed before him—to visit each town in search of Lila, the girl from his past and perhaps from his dreams.

Determined, Aaron embarked on this nationwide quest. His heart wove a pattern of hope and subsequent disappointment with each Harmony visited. The worn photograph of him and Lila was his constant guide, a beacon in his relentless search.

As he reached the halfway point of his journey, fatigue and disillusionment clouded his spirit. The relentless cycle of hopefulness followed by the reality of not finding Lila tested his resolve. In these moments of doubt, the journey felt endless, each town reflecting his growing uncertainty.

However, deep within, a resilient part of Aaron refused to yield to despair. It was an inner conviction, a quiet yet unyielding voice urging him to continue. This inner strength was fueled by the profound experiences and wisdom he had garnered, a belief in the meaningfulness of his path, even in the face of repeated disappointment.

As he visited each town named Harmony, the varied landscape of America unfolded before him, each location offering a unique glimpse into his journey. The photo of him and Lila, marked by the passage of time, had become more than just a picture. It symbolized not only his search for Lila but also represented a deeper desire—a longing for understanding and fulfillment.

In every Harmony, from quiet countrysides to lively urban centers, each setting added its own color. There were small cafes where conversations revealed unexpected wisdom, winding paths that seemed to mirror his coma's adventures and his current uncertain trek. Evenings bathed the surroundings in reflective hues, stirring thoughts of possibilities and 'what could be'. With every person he met, he looked for hints of Lila, yet with each interaction, he discovered deeper parts of his identity. This quest continued to reshape Aaron, each destination solidifying his insights into the complex web of human relationships and his authentic inner landscape.

Driving from one Harmony to the next, the Bronco turned into a sanctuary of introspection, the forward motion echoing the progression of his thoughts and the insights and knowledge gained in the ethereal. His search for Lila was becoming more than a mere quest; it was a continued exploration of self-discovery, with each Harmony representing a meaningful way-point that delved deeper into the essence of searching and, potentially, finding.

As Aaron approached the final few Harmonies on his list, his heart was a swirl of emotions, each town stirring hope and solemnity. Despite Lila's tangible absence, an unyielding conviction drove him onward. This ineffable belief, transcending the realms of logic, whispered of an impending revelation, a culmination of his relentless pursuit.

In the solitude of Harmony, Maine, Aaron delved into introspection. His journey's myriad philosophies and teachings—Buddhism's insights on suffering, Taoism's flow, Existentialism's emphasis on individual meaning, and Hinduism's interconnectedness—swirled together in his mind. They merged into a understanding that his search for Lila was more than a literal pursuit. Lila had become an idea, a concept, a 'Way'. The girl in the photograph, perhaps was just that, a memory. Still, the essence of what she represented was timeless.

In this moment of quietude, Aaron grasped that his journey across the Harmonies of America was less about finding Lila and more about discovering his inner harmony. It was another layer of learning, a realization about acceptance and aligning with life's unfolding, whatever it might bring.

As he left Harmony, Maine, Aaron carried a new perspective. His quest had evolved into an understanding that Lila, whether a person from his past or a symbol of an idea, represented a harmony he could recreate within himself. His journey was not just about a reunion with a long-lost friend; it was about harmonizing with life, embracing its lessons, and finding peace in accepting its mysteries.

Driving away from Maine, Aaron's destination was uncertain. Colorado was in his mind as a possibility. A place where the mountains met the sky, where perhaps he could find a physical manifestation of the harmony he now felt within. Yet, the road ahead was open, a path not just to a place but to a continued journey of self-discovery and understanding.

The journey, Aaron realized, was never about the destination. It was about the lessons learned, the wisdom gained, and the inner peace forged from the fires of his experiences. As he drove, the open road ahead symbolized life's endless possibilities. A journey that continued beyond the pages of his story into the realm of the unknown infinite.

Aaron decided to take the scenic route back west, considering Colorado for its blend of mountains and water. His journey took him to Burlington, Vermont, where fate miraculously intervened.

As Aaron wandered the streets of Burlington, a veil of surrealism draped over his senses. The town, bathed in the soft glow of the setting sun, seemed to exist between reality and the ethereal landscapes of his journey. It was here, amidst this dreamlike ambiance, that his sojourn took yet another turn.

His heart, a fury of emotions, nearly ceased as he stood before a quaint bookstore. The Latin inscription over the door, *In sua voluntade è nostra pace,* resonated with a profound familiarity, echoing a memory from the depths of his dream. With hands trembling, a mix of anticipation and uncertainty coursing through him, Aaron pushed open the door, stepping into a realm that blurred the lines between his past, present, and potential future.

Inside, the bookstore was a sanctuary of knowledge, its walls lined with tomes that whispered tales of ancient wisdom and modern musings. A stately gentleman, his eyes pools of kindness and understanding, greeted Aaron with a smile that seemed to recognize the man before him and the journey he had undertaken.

Wordlessly, Aaron presented the photograph, his fingers clinging to it as if it were a lifeline to his past. The bookstore owner's eyes softened as he gazed at the image. "Wow, look at Lila, so young," he murmured, his voice a gentle breeze in the stillness of the shop. He stretched out his hand to Aaron, "I'm James. Pleased to meet you."

In their brief exchange, James unveiled a truth that set Aaron's heart racing—Lila owned a boarding house on the outskirts of town, Harmony Lane. This revelation was a beacon in the twilight of his journey, illuminating a path that Aaron had both longed for and feared.

With each step towards the boarding house, Aaron's heart mirrored the rhythm of his journey—a crescendo of hope, fear, and profound longing. The streets of Burlington transformed under his feet, each cobblestone, each turn, a metaphor for the winding path of his life.

As he neared the boarding house, nestled amidst a grove of whispering trees, Aaron's thoughts spiraled through the complexities of his journey. The teachings, the philosophies, the myriad encounters—they had all led him here, to this moment, on the threshold of a reunion that was as much about rediscovering himself as it was about finding Lila.

The boarding house, a charming edifice that spoke of stories and lives interwoven within its walls, stood before him. Aaron's breath caught in his throat as he approached, each step heavy with the weight of years and dreams.

Aaron stood on the precipice of a revelation. It was more than a search for a person; it was a search for a connection that transcended time, dreams, and objective reality. The photograph, the Latin inscription, James's recognition—all were threads in the intricate web of his journey.

As he stood there, the door to the boarding house opened, and there she was—Lila. The sight of her, framed in the doorway of a reality he had only dared to hope, was a catharsis that transcended words. In her eyes, he saw not just the girl from the photograph but the embodiment of every lesson, every trial, every step he had taken on his path.

As Lila stood in the doorway, a fleeting sense of familiarity flickered across her face. Her gaze, intermingled with confusion and curiosity, rested on Aaron. "Can I help you?" she asked gently, her voice a melody that resonated with the echoes of a shared past. "Perhaps you're looking for a room?"

Aaron stood overwhelmed with a torrent of emotions. He found himself momentarily voiceless. The journey, the dreams, and the endless time searching had led him to this pivotal moment, yet words eluded him. With trembling hands, he extended the ornate box towards her.

Lila's eyes widened in recognition as she gently took the box. Memories, long buried in the recesses of her childhood, surged forth as she caressed the familiar artifact. She had lost it years ago, a cherished relic of a past that now stood before her, embodied in the man holding out the box.

Lila opened the box with a hesitant touch, revealing the photograph nestled within. Her breath caught as she gazed upon the image of her younger self with Aaron. Lifting her eyes to meet his, a cascade of realizations washed over her. "Aaron?" she whispered. Her voice was a blend of astonishment and dawning recognition.

Tears welled in her eyes as she began to speak, her voice trembling with emotion. "I had this, thing. The coma." she started, her words trailing into the charged air between them.

Aaron, his own eyes brimming with tears, nodded, understanding the depth of what she meant. The journey and the unexplainable connection they shared all converged in this single, profound moment.

They stood there, tears streaming down their faces, as years of separation, longing, and an inexplicable bond culminated in their reunion. The world around them dissipated, leaving only the reality of their shared experience. Their connection defied logic and transcended the boundaries of time and space.

In sua voluntade è nostra pace

Epilogue

A Night by the River

As the river whispered secrets to the night, Aaron and Lila, nestled in their tent, gazed up at the starlit sky. The riverbank, a canvas of their shared memories and miracles, held them in a serene embrace.

Aaron's eyes flickered to the white pickup nearby. "Half a billion in that truck, and it just...appeared?" he mused, half to himself.

"Yes," Lila chuckled, "Just like that. I pulled it in the barn. And then, coma time."

They fell into a contemplative silence, pondering their newfound fortune. "A shelter for veterans, or one for wayward children?" Aaron pondered aloud. "Which do we start with?"

"And, why are we choosing?" Lila responded.

Aaron smiled, "Right. Both!"

Their laughter, light and knowing, danced with the night air, an unspoken acceptance of the surreal tapestry of their lives.

Suddenly, Lila paused. "Is that croaking I hear?" she queried, tilting her head.

Peeking outside, they found themselves amidst a gathering of whimsical, oddly shaped large toads, a scene as inexplicably magical as their own journey, underscoring the night with a playful touch of the extraordinary.

About Dr. Dave Ferruolo

Dr. Dave Ferruolo's life story is one of extraordinary experiences, weaving together the threads of courage, exploration, and psychological depth. His latest work, "Miracle Man," is a compelling embodiment of this richness. A former Navy SEAL, Dr. Dave's firsthand knowledge of military rigors lends a visceral realism to the novel. Transitioning from the elite ranks of the military to the thoughtful corridors of psychotherapy, his journey informs every page with profound psychological insights, particularly into the veteran's psyche.

Holding both a Masters and a Doctorate focusing on veteran mental health, Dr. Dave infuses "Miracle Man" with both academic rigor and heartfelt empathy. His role as a professor of psychology and social work, coupled with his leadership at LifeWorks Counseling Associates, showcases his deep commitment to mental wellness and innovative therapeutic approaches. This blend of real-world experience and scholarly understanding makes the narrative of "Miracle Man" resonate with authenticity and depth.

Beyond his professional accolades, Dr. Dave's philosophy of life is one of a relentless pursuit of knowledge, personal empowerment, and the achievement of Life Success. This philosophy permeates his writing, making "Miracle Man" a beacon of hope and transformation. The novel is not just a journey through the protagonist's trials but also a call to the reader to explore the uncharted territories within themselves. It challenges and inspires, beckoning readers to embark on their own paths of self-discovery, transformation, and resilience.

In "Miracle Man," Dr. Dave Ferruolo offers more than a story; he extends an invitation to join him in a journey of exploration, resilience, and profound human connection. This narrative stands as a testament to the indomitable human spirit, encouraging each reader to blaze their own trail towards healing and fulfillment.

drdavebooks.com

www.ingramcontent.com/pod-product-compliance
Lightning Source LLC
Chambersburg PA
CBHW070715130626
46553CB00005B/1994